The London Look fashion from street to catwalk

The London Look

fashion from street to catwalk

Christopher Breward · Edwina Ehrman · Caroline Evans

Yale University Press

New Haven & London
in association with the

Museum of London

This book has been published in conjunction with the Museum of London exhibition, *The London Look: Fashion from Street to Catwalk*, 29 October 2004 – 8 May 2005.

Supported by A · H · R · B
arts and humanities research board

Museum of London
London Wall
London EC2Y 5HN

Published by Yale University Press in association with the Museum of London

Yale University Press
302 Temple Street, New Haven CT 06511
47 Bedford Square, London WC1B 3DP
www.yale.edu/yup   www.yalebooks.co.uk

Designed by Sally Salvesen
Printed in Italy

LIBRARY OF CONGRESS CATALOGING-IN-PUBLICATION DATA

Breward, Christopher, 1965–
  The London look: fashion from street to catwalk /
Christopher Breward, Edwina Ehrman, Caroline Evans.
     p. cm.
  Includes bibliographical references and index.
  ISBN 0-300-10399-9 (cl : alk. paper)
        0-904818-87-x (paper : museum edition)
  1. Clothing trade–England–London–History. 2. Fashion–
England–London–History. 3. Costume–England–London–
History. I. Ehrman, Edwina. II. Evans, Caroline. III. Title.

TT496.G72L663 2004
391′.009421--dc22

                                  2004009135

ILLUSTRATIONS

Frontispiece: Finale of Alexander McQueen's autumn/winter 1998 show (see fig. 155). Photograph by Niall McInerney.

Cover: (*front*) The New Look: Wenda Rogerson and Barbara Goalen wearing Hardy Amies and Molyneux coats, photographed by Norman Parkinson, March 1949 (© Norman Parkinson Ltd); (*back*) Silk satin embroidered waistcoat, 1850s (top left). Ribbed wool New Look coat, spring 1949, designed by Hardy Amies (top right). Denim jacket, *c.*1980, customised with a crucifix image and Oi! slogans (bottom left). Biba trouser suit, *c.*1973 (bottom right).

CONTENTS

ACKNOWLEDGEMENTS

Christopher Breward and Caroline Evans would like to thank the Arts and Humanities Research Board of Great Britain for supporting their work on this book and the accompanying exhibition as part of the AHRB-funded project 'Fashion and Modernity', running between 2001 and 2004 at Central Saint Martins College of Art and Design and the London College of Fashion. Christopher Breward also notes the support he has received from the ESRC/AHRB 'Cultures of Consumption' programme (project RES-143-25-0038) to complete research on London's fashion cultures.

The authors would also like to extend their special thanks to Oriole Cullen at the Museum of London whose unstinting support and expertise have contributed so much to this book and the exhibition, and to Helen Ganiaris who oversaw the project at the Museum. We are also grateful to Rose Brown, Nicola Dunn, Jane Lewis, Anna Mastromina, Catherine Nightingale and Deborah Phipps in the Conservation Department; to Hilary Davidson and Kirsti Wilkinson for their help preparing mannequins for photography; to John Chase, Torla Evans and Richard Stroud in the Photography Department; to Maggie Cox and to Julie Cochrane and Anna Wright in the Picture Library.

In addition we would like to thank Rebecca Arnold, Katherine Baird and staff at the London College of Fashion Library; Randy Bigham; Andrew Bolton; Sally Brooks; Anna Buruma and Liberty PLC; Madeleine Ginsburg and the DAKS/Simpson Archive; Diana Haber; Sandra Holtby; Amy de la Haye; Lucy Johnston; Heather Lambert; Jenny Lister; Dr Robert Lutton; Phyllis Magidson; staff at the Victoria & Albert Museum (Archive of Art & Design); Alistair O'Neill; Christopher Phipps and staff at the London Library; Clare Rose; Cathy Ross; Roger Sabin; Mike Seaborne; Calum Storrie; June Swann; Marketa Uhlirova and Jennifer Weardon.

Finally we would like to express our gratitude to Tracy Wellman, the Museum of London Publications Officer; and to our editors, Mark Kilfoyle, and Sally Salvesen at Yale University Press.

FOREWORD

By definition, fashion leads. A fashion that follows is no fashion at all. It is behind the time, out of date. Fashion must be of the moment for its impact, its very impulse, to thrive.

What is it about London that makes it such a compelling fashion city? One proof immediately springs to mind: the capital's celebrated Savile Row traditions which honour the past as famously as do the fashion cultures of Paris, say, or Milan. Yet London too is of the moment. Its mad urban maelstrom of invention easily matches the cutting-edge spirit of new fashion centres such as Tokyo and Shanghai. Fashion becomes one lens through which to see the city's modern identity, one in which London is, always, embedded in a world history and caught up in the excitement of a global future. It is a future in which the London look is always changing.

Standing in the exhibition which this book accompanies, you can see the city's diversity on show. If imperial contact brought a wealth of new ideas, skills and perceptions, Londoners absorbed the world's varieties and made them their own. From Liberty fabrics to the shops of Berwick Street, the sheer tumult of London speaks to alternative styles and new fusions, holding on to something 'other', making something new. It is, *par excellence*, a city in love with diversity and cocky enough to thumb its nose at what's proper.

As so many fashionable looks have shown – from Regency dandies to sixties Mods – mixing and matching is what marks the city as a perennial playground of styles and cultures. That is why so many artists and designers choose to live in London. And it is a fair exchange for the vast number of London fashion designers who move to Paris and New York with skills, ideas and a freshness of approach that sets London apart. With such diverse input, the London look is a hundred different things at once. That is why it travels: it is fascinating itself, because it is fascinated with the world.

Professor Jack Lohman
Director
Museum of London

INTRODUCTION *Christopher Breward*

London looms large in the imaginations of political philosophers, economists, architects, historians, writers and artists as the quintessential, all-consuming city. For centuries – alongside its status as a centre of national and colonial government, international trade and financial speculation – the capital's huge physical size, its extremes of wealth and poverty, its shifting and variegated population, its deep sense of the past and sharp hunger for the future have all helped to position London as first among a succession of thriving world cities. The fortunes of these cities have profoundly informed the nature of modern civilisation.

Yet among its contributions to modern culture, who would credit London for its sartorial success? Most observers would surely argue that London's identity is bound up with the sooty grandeur of its public institutions, its commercial competitiveness and its diverse population, not the style of its inhabitants' dress. For many the appeal of the capital lies in the structures of its official landscape: the Tower of London, St Paul's, the Houses of Parliament, Buckingham Palace. If clothing features at all in the symbolic imagery of London, it is perhaps in its clichéd 'official' forms: as ceremonial garb for guardsmen and beefeaters, or uniforms for policemen and bowler-hatted office workers. Despite the occasional, uncharacteristic moment of frenetic activity, such as the 'swinging sixties', when fashion does appear in the familiar stories of the city, it is often as an 'out of place' concept, seemingly more suited to the style-driven cultures of Paris, Milan or New York.

Yet far from endorsing the conventional thinking that sees fashion as an alien intrusion into the life of London, this book and the exhibition at the Museum of London to which it closely relates argue that the design, manufacture, retailing and use of fashionable dress in the capital have always played a vital role in forming London's distinctive character. The evidence is striking. The trades set up to clothe London's population since its earliest days have defined the city's complex physical and economic geography in as fundamental a manner as any number of official plans or council edicts. The manner in which Londoners have displayed their social status and taste through their personal clothing has left a mark on the city's interiors, streets, parks and squares as definite as any architectural detailing or traffic flow. In fact, as a barometer of prevailing economic and aesthetic trends and political and social pressures, fashion is as sensitive a record of change in an urban context as bricks and mortar or government statistics. And if fashion has been overlooked, it is because its ephemeral nature renders the evidence of fashion tantalisingly fragile and fragmentary, qualities that have placed it out of the reach of most mainstream historians of the city.[1]

FASHION CITIES

London's prominence as a global fashion city has perhaps been eclipsed by the attention given to more stereotypical, self-promoting centres of sartorial creativity. Any attempt to chart fashion's defining role in the modern metropolis requires a consideration of factors that have brought clothing into play with other forms of urban material culture across the globe. In such a reading, London can be seen to share historical continuities and circumstances with more celebrated fashion capitals such as Paris, Milan and New York, or more recently Tokyo and

Fig. 1 Skinheads and hippies, Piccadilly Circus, detail of fig. 10.

Fig. 2   Soho, *Master Map of Poverty*, 1889. Charles Booth (1840–1916). Booth's map is an early example of social cartography. Each street is coloured to indicate the income and social class of its inhabitants. The blue areas denote poverty, with dark blue indicating chronic want.

Fig. 3   Coiffeur, boulevard de Strasbourg, 1912. Photograph by Eugène Atget (1857–1927). (Copyright George Eastman House)

Antwerp. The first fashion centres – fifteenth-century Venice, Florence, Paris, Bruges and London – prospered through the textile trade and the proximity of a thriving court culture where the display of luxury was a political necessity. By the eighteenth century, the expansion of economic and military networks to incorporate new empires facilitated the exchange of raw materials, organisation of labour and the opening of markets on an unprecedented scale. For European fashion cities, which now included Brussels, Berlin and Vienna alongside London, Rome and Paris, the opportunities for growth were limitless. Modish clothing joined state ceremonial, architectural planning, artistic patronage and tourism as a vital currency in the competitive display between nations, though nowhere was the promotion of luxurious dress more marked than in Paris (fig. 3).[2]

By the early twentieth century, New York had evolved as a transatlantic challenge to the supremacy of its older European sisters. New York's fashion district provided democratic garments to a growing American market no longer constrained by the hierarchical social structures of the old world. It was aided by new production technologies which were fast overtaking the rate of innovation in Europe. More importantly, New York and then Los Angeles dealt in the new mass-production of images through magazines and film. Their impact elevated the symbolic importance of the fashion city above its capacity to produce and export actual clothes. In this scenario, the equation of urban life with modishness informed the presentation of Paris and New York as stereotypically spectacular fashion centres in luxury product advertising, Hollywood melodramas and *Vogue* photographic shoots alike (fig. 4).[3]

London found a niche in this new landscape as the bastion either of tradition (Savile Row) or subversion (Carnaby Street). The city was to be joined in the final decades of the twentieth century by Milan – where the flexibility and high production values of the northern Italian textile industry enabled Milan to overtake Rome as the centre of Italian glamour culture – and Tokyo, where a similar combination of traditional craft skills and futuristic technologies were bolstered by a youthful consumer society hungry for new products (fig. 5).[4] New locations for the celebration of fashion culture are constantly emerging, with Shanghai and Antwerp most recently attracting attention for, respectively, an aggressive enthusiasm for new production and marketing techniques engineered to serve the largest emerging market in modern history; and a more self-conscious reflection by local designers, curators and journalists on the uses of avant-garde fashion design as a motor for urban regeneration through the mobilisation of media and museum initiatives.

In the twenty-first century, London's reputation as a guardian of the bespoke and the edgy remains a constant in a longstanding, international configuration of fashion cities. But this shared history, in which similarities with other centres come naturally to the fore, perhaps obscures the particular characteristics which have always drawn attention to London as a very singular, but sometimes overlooked, example of the fashion city phenomenon.[5] In seeking to define these characteristics, we can identify four key organisational categories in which the material qualities, symbolic meanings and popular appeal of London fashions have at different moments offered a distinctive, but sometimes chaotic and cross-cutting, sartorial vision, quite at

Fig. 4   The casual 'New York look'. Photograph by Vernon Merritt, 1 January 1969.(Copyright Time Life).

Fig. 5   Tokyo street style, *FRUiTS* magazine, 1998. Photograph by Shoichi Aoki. (Copyright FRUiTS/Shoichi Aoki).

Fig. 6   Bespoke surtout (overcoat), c.1843. Made of British wool facecloth for John Francis Close (1802–58). Close was British consul at Tournay Charente from 1830.

odds with the more controlled self-presentations of other fashion centres. This vision can be summarised as a parallel concern with tradition, innovation, the 'alternative', and stylistic fusion in fashionable dress. These interlinking obsessions weave through the chronology of development and adaptation presented in the chapters that follow.

TRADITION

The idea that London is a world centre for the production and retailing of traditional fashion goods is a relatively recent one. It coincides ironically with the reinvention of the city as a fulcrum for modernity in the early eighteenth century. Prior to this, in the sixteenth and seventeenth centuries, most luxury goods that have since become associated with the capital – fine

Fig. 7   A workroom at John Lobb Ltd,
9 St James's Street, London, 1988.
The bootmakers was founded in 1849.

leather goods, accessories and fashionable tailoring – came from abroad. As historian Francis Sheppard notes, London's 'role on the international scene [in this earlier period] was analogous to that of her own colonies in later years, selling primary or unfinished products to more advanced economies and buying manufactured goods in exchange'.[6] Only the semi-permanent arrival of the aristocracy in town and the formalisation of the social season created the large and reliable market upon which manufacturers and traders in fine bespoke goods depended.

The raw materials from which these goods were constructed – precious metals, hides, linens and woollen cloth – had thus long been traded in the capital and were the basis of the city's prosperity. But it was gradually the skill in their finishing that drew the attention of consumers (fig. 6). The forms taken by London's 'traditional' products also owe a great deal to the lifestyles of their original patrons: their craving for a subtle code of social distinction that protected their interests and discouraged crude imitation. The functional solidity of a bespoke shoe or suit, combined with its understated but exquisite detail, betrays an aristocratic heritage. It was a heritage rooted practically in rural pursuits, which occupied the landed classes for the half of the year in which they attended to their country estates, and psychologically in the observance of social niceties that were strictly metropolitan in focus.

The predictable annual cycle of court, parliament and socialising which constituted the 'season', together with the concentration of aristocratic households in the West End, further informed the nature of a bespoke trade. This trade supported long-established family firms well able to command consumer loyalty and maintain discreet central London locations. This carefully guarded network of supply – with its distinctive terminology, understated trademarks and specialist skills – has survived (at least partially) into the present, and imparts that archaic aura and adherence to old-fashioned values of service and high standards that still signify 'London' to

a majority of well-heeled consumers. Largely oriented towards a masculine audience and deeply implicated in the conservative values of the British class-system, London's traditional fashion economy has nevertheless exerted a far-reaching influence on the direction and understanding of London style over the past two centuries. It has produced the Savile Row tailored suit, the Jermyn Street shirt and hand-made brogue, and the St James's Street bowler hat which have signified urbane sophistication for almost two centuries (fig. 7).

INNOVATION

Fig. 8   Moss crêpe evening dress, with detail, c.1970. Designed by Ossie Clark.

Balancing the dominant impulses of the traditionalists, and sometimes subverting them to startling effect, the opposite tendency within London's fashion cultures has been towards creative

Fig. 9 Outfit from Boudicca's Hunter-Gatherer collection, autumn/winter 2004. Zowie Broach and Brian Kirkby of the London label Boudicca are known for their non-conformist, conceptual approach to fashion. Catwalk photography by Chris Moore. (Copyright Boudicca).

Fig. 10   A gang of skinheads passing a group of hippies, Piccadilly Circus, 1969. Photograph by Terry Spencer. (Copyright Terry Spencer).

practices that are socially, technologically or aesthetically innovative. In its earlier history, the city was not noted for the manufacture of particularly rare or unusual clothing products. From the early eighteenth century, the scale of production in London was remarkable, exceeding that of any foreign competitor. The organisation and range of labour skills in the capital offered greater scope for innovation rather than production techniques or product styles. One negative consequence of this was that 'sweating' became a problem particularly associated with London in the nineteenth century. In a more positive sense, London's huge and adaptable pool of skills, strong communication links with the rest of the country and the world, and ready access to markets and cash has meant that the capital has been able to support the trial and introduction of several technically innovative fashion commodities, from ready-made clothing to waterproofed garments to synthetic dyes.

Other examples of innovation lie in London's unique provision for fashion education. Admittedly, specific state-supported vocational courses on manufacturing techniques were not made available in the city until the early twentieth century at the London College of Fashion. Before then, those seeking a career in the industry relied on trade apprenticeships and the limited scope of private needlework schools. From the mid-twentieth century, courses in fashion design at the Royal College of Art and St Martin's School of Art formed the foundation for London's reputation as a forcing house for creative talent in this field. Students from Ossie Clark in the 1960s (fig. 8) to Hussein Chalayan in the 1990s benefited from a forward-looking design education in which visual research and creative expression were valued as highly as technical or business skills. This embrace of the avant-garde and interdisciplinary in London's famous art colleges was matched by opportunities on offer to all in London's streets and clubs. There the multi-

Fig. 11 'Noon', *The Four Times of the Day*, 1738. Engraving after William Hogarth (1697–1764) from *The Works of William Hogarth from the original plates restored by James Heath Esq., R.A.*, 1822.

Fig. 12   Quilted and embroidered silk dressing jacket made in Japan for the western market, c.1898. Liberty's of Regent Street offered jackets very similar to this in their Christmas catalogue for 1898.

layered pasts of a world city have inspired generations of aspiring designers, retailers and commentators to produce challenging interpretations of contemporary life through the medium of fashion.

ALTERNATIVE STYLES

It is perhaps in the theatrical milieu of the street that London fashion has really achieved a world-renowned distinctiveness. In recent decades this has been manifested most strongly through the dress of the young. Successive subcultural groups – from the Teddy boys of south and east London, through the Mods of Carnaby Street, to the Punks and New Romantics of the King's Road – have seized the capital as a stage for acts of sartorial delinquency (fig. 10). While the globalisation of fashion production and consumption has rendered such spectacles less shocking, London is still associated by editors, stylists and trend-seekers with an edgy, amateurish grit in which the idiosyncratic is rated over the dominance of international brands and homogenising high-street chains. Indeed, young Londoners are often applauded for their ability to take these global trends and reinvent them in a satirical vein.

The concept of the city as a repository of inspirational imagery, rags and ephemera rich in transformative potential is, however, older than the post-war youth culture boom of the 1950s, 60s and 70s. London's longer fashion history is punctuated by a series of strikingly theatrical stereotypes. These fashion performers found that the lively public culture of the capital offered a backdrop and an audience, as well as a certain freedom to test boundaries, while safely ensconcing them in the anonymity that a major city also provides. The rakes, fops and macaronis of eighteenth-century London used the extreme fringes of fashion culture for the exaggerated tailoring, cosmetics and wigs that constituted their highly politicised affront to the status quo (fig. 11). The print and coffee shops which supported their masquerades were gradually replaced by the gentlemen's clubs and sporting venues of Regency London. These too became arenas for the posturing of the dandy, that embodiment of urbane sophistication and retrograde snobbery. In the late nineteenth century, the romantic impulse of dandyism was transformed again through the aesthetic and bohemian dressing associated with the circle of Oscar Wilde, while the flapper or 'London girl' of the 1920s demonstrated the ease with which a glamorous sense of modernity, inspired by film, theatre and the promises of a revived consumer culture, was achievable even by those on limited means.

FUSION

Diverse ethnic communities have always featured as a distinctive element of London's demographic make-up. The city's status as the centre of empire drew groups who, from the eighteenth to the twentieth century, have made a definably strong contribution to the developing iconography of London fashions. The resulting fusion of traditions and styles – based on ideas of trade, exchange, travel and sometimes conflict – has been a constant theme in London fashion, producing both an excitingly performative sense of London style at different moments and a strong rejoinder to any description of fashion which limits itself to fixed notions of location, history, culture and identity. With this in mind, it is possible to claim that a wide range of styles and garments – an 1860s Zouave jacket purchased in Oxford Street (fig. 40); a Liberty Japanese dressing jacket of the 1890s (fig. 12); peasant-inspired Knightsbridge embroideries of the 1920s; the fey orientalism of Bill Gibb and Thea Porter prevalent in the 1970s; the globally influenced collections of contemporary designers such as Sophia Kokosalaki (fig. 158) and Maharishi – are quintessentially 'of London' in approach and appeal. London style looks to be as much a matter of mind-set and orientation, the creation of a particular 'look', as it is the simple issue of origination.

PREHISTORIES

This book and the exhibition it accompanies focus on the development of a London look over the last two centuries. This is not to argue that the conditions supporting the rise of recognisable London fashions, or the wearing of garments distinctive to the capital, emerged only after 1800.

VAUXHALL GARDENS, shewing the Grand Walk, at the entrance of the Garden, and the Orchestra, with the Musick Playing.   La Grande Allée a l'entrée des JARDINS de VAUXHALL, L'Orchestra, et les Musiciens.

Printed for John Bowles & Son, at the Black Horse in Cornhil.

Fig. 13   *Vauxhall Gardens, shewing the Grand Walk*, 1751. Hand-coloured engraving by J. S. Muller (1715–post-1785) after S. Wale (d. 1786).

Travellers' accounts, images, inventories, official records and the evidence of surviving clothing itself all point to the existence of a thriving fashion culture in London since the beginnings of modern fashion.[7] London's reputation as a city with a distinctive and profitable sartorial style coincides with its transformation as a world city in the late modern period.

That said, the preconditions for this transformation were well in place by the dawn of the nineteenth century. From the mid-sixteenth to the early eighteenth century, the population of the capital had increased sevenfold from about 75,000 to 575,000 inhabitants. This expansion stimulated consumer demand, investment, specialisation and trade, and consolidated the attraction which Parliament, court and the *beau monde* brought to the city.[8] The production of clothing for all stations of society accounted for a considerable proportion of manufacturing activity in London well before the rise of sweating in the mid-nineteenth century. Outnumbering male tailors of outerwear, thousands of women worked in the capital during the eighteenth century to produce hooped petticoats, shirts, shifts, gowns, cloaks, stockings, wigs and hats. Much of this labour was carried out at home for piece rates, and though demand could be high, it was also seasonal and prone to fluctuations in taste, leading to successive periods of exhausting overwork and damaging unemployment. Not for nothing did the clothing industries of London gain the negative description, the 'rag trade'.

Echoing this scale of manufacturing activity was London's well-established reputation as a national and international centre for shopping well before the metropolitan improvements of the early nineteenth century. The German visitor Sophie von la Roche left a highly evocative description of a trip to Oxford Street in 1786:

> Just imagine a street taking half an hour to cover from end to end, with double rows of shining lamps, in the middle of which stands an equally long row of beautifully lacquered coaches . . . and the pavement, inlaid with flagstones, can stand six people deep and allows one to gaze at the splendidly lit shop fronts in comfort. First one passes a watchmaker's, then a silk or fan store, now a silversmith's, a china or glass shop . . .[9]

The opulence that von la Roche describes in the retail sector was also to be found in the fields of public and private entertainment. By the 1780s, aristocratic houses, assembly rooms, theatres and pleasure gardens in London had become renowned across Europe for their lavish provision (fig. 13). Funded by the profits of trade and colonisation in India and the West Indies, the glittering consumption of Georgian London sat cheek by jowl with unprecedented poverty, squalor and overcrowding. This opposition is typical of London's emerging identity as a city marked by chaos, vitality and sharply contrasting sensations. As the following chapters suggest, one effect of this enduring context is that it ensures the survival of a thriving fashion culture replicated nowhere else on earth.

GENTLEFOLK IN TOWN: 1800–30 *Christopher Breward*

In 1823 the Marquise de Vermont and Sir Charles Darnley (a pseudonymous pair of authors representing the views of the quintessential French aristocratic and the English gentleman abroad) shared their experiences of travel in London and Paris. Their tourist guide of the two cities celebrated London's new-found superiority over her old rival as a world city of taste and style. De Vermont railed impotently at the extreme fashion sense of his recently adopted home:

> The most tyrannical uniformity is exacted in London . . . wearing a hat an inch too wide in the brim, a waistcoat too short, or a coat too long, subjects the unfortunate and unconscious foreigner to a suspicion of vulgarity quite sufficient to banish him from the elegant circles of this gay metropolis. I have therefore begun my career by completely new modelling my costume, and for that purpose have put myself in the hands of the most celebrated professors. My hair has been cut by Blake, my waistcoat and pantaloons come from the hands of artists of equal celebrity, each devoted to the particular line of his profession. Lock is my hatter and Hoby my shoemaker; and . . . a kind English friend has taught me . . . how to obtain a perfect tie. Indeed, I am so metamorphosed that you would scarcely recognise me. I can now pass unquizzed through a crowd of dandies; and I even had, a few days since, the glory of overhearing one of the most renowned of these heroes express his approbation of the brilliant polish which my boots displayed.[1]

As de Vermont's description suggests, London's inhabitants, especially its wealthy young men, emerged in the 1810s and 1820s as a recognisable group of style-obsessives. The historian Roy Porter argued that this revolutionary generation of trendsetters 'forged an aesthetic of the urban, a worship of town as a temple of pleasure that culminated in the image of the dandy'. This new mode of dressing and behaviour 'gave urban lifestyles a glamour that became the envy, or amusement, of the rest of the nation', positioning fashionable Londoners as 'city watchers, self-referential . . . in love with themselves'.[2] Such a refashioning was echoed during the period by a transformation in the architectural back-drop of the capital, a process which ensured that the posturing of the new fashion consumer took place on an appropriately dressed stage. As is often the case in London's sartorial history, the development of clothing and buildings were closely intertwined.

THE NEW WEST END: A THEATRE OF FASHION

The West End of London was the capital's most prestigious fashionable district from the start. It grew piecemeal from the late seventeenth century, filling a relative no-man's land between the grand classical palaces and parks of the nobility that followed the course of Piccadilly to the south, and the more commercial thoroughfare of Oxford Street to the north. St James's Fields was among the first of a series of residential developments designed to provide a permanent city residence for the great country landowners, who were also keen to maximise the rental income of their London estates. As the eighteenth century progressed, the gabled evidence of country life and the scrubby hinterlands of small-scale manufacturing, which survived beyond the new squares and Palladian mansions, were obliterated by rows of brick terraces accented by mass-produced classical detailing. Increasing numbers of lesser country gentry decamped to these elegant

Fig. 14 *The Quadrant, Regent Street,* 1822. Aquatint by J. Bluck (fl. 1791–1831) after Thomas Hosmer Shepherd (1793–1864).

Fig. 15   *Burlington Arcade*, 1828.
Engraving by William Tombleson
(b. *c.*1795) after Thomas Hosmer
Shepherd (1793–1864).

terraces in emulation of their aristocratic betters. By the second decade of the next century, the demolition necessary for the building of Regent Street, designed by John Nash as the premier purpose-built shopping promenade in Europe, scythed through the district from the new Regent's Park in the north to Carlton House in the south, imposing a physical and psychological boundary between the genteel concentration of fashionable life to the west and the noisier domain of manufacture and trade in Soho to the east (fig. 14). Completed in 1820, the graceful curve of palace-like shops with their expansive display windows, stuccoed upper-chambers and dramatic focal points (colonnades, circuses and picturesque churches were interspersed with retail premises), set a precedent for the organisation of fashion shopping as a leisure pursuit that would dominate urban planning for decades to come.[3]

A network of smaller shopping streets connected the desires and necessities of an affluent population to the goods pouring out of the new docks upriver. Consumption and display were deeply embedded within the daily life of the community. Three streets in particular served this new metropolitan constituency – Old Bond Street, St James's Street and Savile Row. They converged roughly at Burlington House, adjacent to which Lord George Cavendish's Burlington Arcade was erected in 1818 (fig. 15). The arcade itself was a symbol of the sophisticated marketplace that London had now become. Built by the architect Samuel Ware, its restrained arrangement of ground floor shops was arranged, according to the words of the builder's prospectus, as 'a Piazza for all Hardware, Wearing Apparel and Articles not Offensive in appearance nor smell', protected from the elements by a pitched glass roof.[4] However, above the tiny bow-fronted boutiques (several of which supported millinery businesses), a series of first-floor domestic suites accessed from staircases within the shops rapidly gained a risqué reputation as brothels, providing personal services to the single gentlemen renting chambers in nearby Albany, a luxurious development of purpose-built bachelor chambers erected on the other side of Burlington House in 1804. Licentious aristocratic pleasures, genteel architecture and shopping for fashion cohered in a physical realisation of London's modern attractions.[5]

To the immediate west of the arcade, running north from Piccadilly at the site of the former Clarendon House (demolished in 1686), Old Bond Street was the most established of London's new shopping streets. Its origins lay in the speculative developments of Sir Thomas Bond in the late seventeenth century. By 1700 its length had extended to Clifford Street, where it became New Bond Street, finally meeting Oxford Street in 1721. By the 1820s it was a thriving thoroughfare

Fig. 16   Man's blue cloth tailcoat made by an unknown tailor. The date 1828 has been inscribed in ink on the lining of one of the sleeves.

Fig. 17   Orthopaedic slippers made of gold tissue and lined with silk, *c.*1830. These luxurious slippers, whose soles have been moulded to support the arches of the feet, are said to have been made for King George IV by Mr White of King Street, Westminster.

that included military and civilian tailors, milliners, gunsmiths, bootmakers, hosiers, perfumiers, hatters, wine and coffee merchants, dairymen, bakers, butchers and fishmongers, carpet and china dealers, upholsterers, lamp sellers, coach builders, print sellers, picture dealers and book men. As Old Bond Street segued into New, dressing-case makers, jewellers, a saddler, a horse hirer, an umbrella manufacturer, watchmakers, cutlers, antique dealers and tobacconists ensured that no genteel wish was overlooked. Together, the two Bond streets provided everything requisite to the local man of fashion.[6]

To the south of Piccadilly, St James's Street presented a more conservative interpretation of fashionability. Essentially a street of ultra-respectable gentlemen's clubs and august providers of traditional fare to the royal family (fig. 17), its tenants became more closely associated with the political and social old-guard as the eighteenth century declined. By the 1820s, only the hatter James Lock survived as a modish retreat, as men of fashion including George Brummell, Charles Fox and the Prince Regent extended their patronage northwards.[7] The rise of Savile Row and its neighbourhood as a focus of fine tailoring in the early nineteenth century was partly responsible for this shift in allegiances.

Savile Row was, at this stage, a residential street and enjoyed no particular reputation for retailing. Any notoriety that it did enjoy was a consequence of its eccentric tenants: the bawdy Lord Barrymore, a Byronic monster famed for his shows of horsemanship, directed a private theatre there from the 1790s at which actors and proto-celebrities including Edmund Kean, the Kembles, Richard Sheridan and Lord Byron himself engaged in amateur dramatics. A newcomer to town, seeking the attention of the tailors who in the twenty-first century line both sides of the row, would have been disappointed in his searches, for in the early nineteenth century, tailors mostly visited the homes of their aristocratic clients, rendering the need for a shopfront irrelevant. The tailoring itself – the cutting, stitching, steaming and pressing – was hidden in basements and back rooms, reinforcing the social apartheid imposed by the building of Regent Street in the 1820s and the resulting relegation of industry to the cheap rents and plentiful labour of Soho. Tailors existed in the neighbourhood, but their reputations were built discreetly by word of mouth rather than through flashy window displays; the concept of trade promotion was restricted to the flaunting of ostentatious tailoring on the back of some appropriately titled customer. In this context, the tight concentration of such famous tailors as Meyer of Conduit Street, Schweitzer and Davidson of Cork Street, Weston of Old Bond Street, and Schultz of Clifford Street within the confines of the Old Burlington Estate was unsurprising. Success in the trade clearly relied on the tailor's close proximity to the social haunts and habits of the rich, and an intimate understanding of prevailing aristocratic tastes.[8]

When, in 1821, the journalist Pierce Egan produced his popular print celebration, *Life in London*, he was reflecting the new London culture represented by Meyer, Schultz and their peers. Through the adventures of its heroes Jerry Hawthorne and Corinthian Tom, the book revealed the diversity of a newly confident city: its high and low cultures, its propensity for supporting the reinvention of character, generally via the powers of a nascent consumer culture. So appealing was the world painted by Egan that its episodes were adapted for the stage in four different versions, the most successful running at the Adelphi Theatre for more than three hundred performances.[9] At the level of the street, in the real world, the book's message found material endorsement in a West End transformed by the power of fashion and shopping. As Egan himself enthused, 'the metropolis is a complete CYCLOPAEDIA, wherein every man of the most religious or moral habits, attached to any sect, may find something to please his palate, regulate his taste, suit his pocket, enlarge his mind, and make himself happy and comfortable'.[10]

DRESSING THE DANDY

A key scene in Egan's *Life in London* depicted Jerry Hawthorne being fitted for a new suit by the Regent Street tailor Richard Primefit. Jerry is Corinthian Tom's country cousin, and the acquisition of a set of appropriate West End clothes marks his entry into Tom's exclusive metropolitan milieu. The fitting, recorded in an illustration by the caricaturist Robert Cruikshank, takes place in Tom's apartments, their walls hung with hunting and sporting scenes (fig. 18). Tom sits dressed

Fig. 18   'Jerry in training for a "swell" ',
Life in London, 1821. Pierce Egan
(1772–1849). Drawing and engraving by
Robert (1789–1856) and George
Cruikshank (1792–1878).

in a fashionable oriental dressing gown over the new full-length pantaloons and surveys the action as the dextrous tailor runs his measuring tape over Jerry's broad country back. His cousin wears the functional country uniform of a woollen coat with brass buttons, buff-coloured breeches and white stockings, his own look in effect repromoted by Beau Brummell, the most celebrated of the dandies, as a badge of good taste at the turn of the century. At a table-leg are propped the hessian boots which added a frisson of equestrian and military glamour to this most English of looks.

A double-breasted greatcoat refined to suit city pavements rather than country lanes, survives in the collection of the Museum of London (fig. 19). It was tailored in dark blue face-cloth by John Weston of 34 Old Bond Street in 1803 and conforms well to the properties expected of attire suitable for 'rambling' in the shopping streets of Mayfair and St James, or taking the reins in Hyde Park. Certainly Weston's reputation as tailor and draper to the Prince of Wales and the Dukes of Cambridge, Sussex and Gloucester position him as a master of urbane clothing design. His coat boasts a high-fastening dark blue velvet collar, a figure-hugging cut in which the fine cloth closely caresses the shoulders and torso and flares gracefully to a long skirt, and eight pairs of large gilt buttons made by the London-based metal worker Charles Jennens. Its style naturally borrows from army uniform, in this period dominated by the wars with France during which the trappings of martial swagger could suggest patriotic bravado. As Aileen Ribeiro comments with reference to the similar contemporary fashion for frogging and braid in men's dress: 'Hussar regiments wore some of the most dashing uniforms during the Napoleonic period and it was inevitable that some of this glamour rubbed off onto civilian clothing.'[11] As the century progressed, this vision of patriotic masculinity was to find its virility challenged by a series of refinements which positioned the London dandy as the most artificial and mannered of creatures. As Egan observed in relation to Jerry's transformation :

> During the time Mr Primefit was applying the measure to ascertain the frame of young Hawthorne, the Corinthian smiled to himself at the lusty, unsubdued back of his merry rustic coz., at the same time making comparisons, in his own mind at the vast difference of the hinder parts of his dandy-like friends at the west-end of town, when put into the scale against the country breed of Jerry. Tom laughingly told Primefit that he had not been so well backed for a long time.[12]

Besides the attentions of the tailor, the dandy also relied on the expertise of the hosier for the creation of an appropriate London look, one that emphasised the more flamboyant nature of dandy fashions. The adoption of increasingly complex neckties by fashionable young men in the 1810s and 1820s swiftly attracted the attention of satirists and caricaturists. Brummell's own legend revolved around a description of his morning dressing rituals, whereby his valet would present a gathered audience of friends and followers with Brummell's failed knots on a silver platter – evidence of the master's perfectionism in matters of the wardrobe. His biographer Captain Jesse recorded such a performance:

> The collar, which was always fixed to his shirt, was so large that before being folded down, it completely hid his head and face, and the white neckcloth was at least a foot in height. The first *coup d'archet* was made with the shirt collar, which he folded down to its proper size; and Brummell then standing before the glass with his chin poked up to the ceiling, by the gentle and gradual declension of his lower jaw, creased the cravat to reasonable dimensions, the form of each succeeding crease being perfected with the shirt.[13]

In 1818 the semi-humorous tract, *Neckclothitania, or Tietania: being an essay on starchers, by One of the Cloth*, depicted countless variations on tying a cravat in the manner of a scientific and philo-

Fig. 19   Man's greatcoat, 1803. Made by John Weston of Old Bond Street. A letter from the tailor accompanying the coat described it as 'an exceed[ingly] good blue cloth great coat . . . made in ev[e]ry respect in the best manner'.

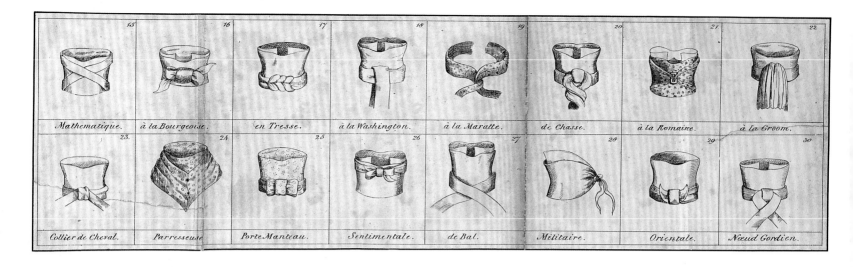

Mathématique. | *à la Bourgeoise.* | *en Tresse.* | *à la Washington.* | *à la Maratte.* | *de Chasse.* | *à la Romaine.* | *à la Groom.*

Collier de Cheval. | *Parresseuse.* | *Porte-Manteau.* | *Sentimentale.* | *de Bal.* | *Militaire.* | *Orientale.* | *Nœud Gordien.*

Fig. 20   Plate B from *The Art of Tying the Cravat*, 7th edition, 1829.

Fig. 21 a and b   Embroidered silk net dress with court train, 1814–16. Associated with Princess Charlotte of Wales.

Detail of the hem: the bellflowers are made using silk-covered wire and net decorated with silk thread darning. The beads are made of blown glass.

sophical treatise. Styles such as the 'oriental', 'mathematical', 'ball room', 'horse collar' and 'maharaja' constructed in various colours and textiles, and starched to greater or lesser degrees, betrayed by their exotic titles the range of interests and experiences available to the man about town (fig. 20). That such trends served to support the expansion of London's fashion trades in a material sense is clearly conveyed by the content of the anonymously authored *Memoirs of a Rambler* published in 1800. In this a Mr Dimity, a Piccadilly hosier, is introduced as an astute businessman, trading on the gullibility of the consumer as a means of supporting his own lavish lifestyle. Faddishness had become a key driver for the metropolitan economy:

> On my first coming to this dealer in white ties and white linen, he took me aside and with much earnestness observed: 'It has always been my ambition to employ sharp cunning fellows in my shop, I therefore trust that you will observe the established maxims so strictly adhered to by all snippers of muslin and clippers of cambric, which are: "take in everybody as you can, but suffer nobody to take you in. Deal pretty much in the marvellous, and always make two prices." For if it were not for these things, how should my neighbour Froth, the haberdasher, keep his gig and country house at Newington Butts, or I my one horse chaise and villa at Hammersmith?'[14]

WOMEN'S FASHIONS IN LONDON

Women shoppers had, of course, long been represented as the dupes of unscrupulous London clothing and textile traders in caricature and satire. But the ubiquitous presence of the male dandy in the early nineteenth century temporarily eclipsed the women's role as the leading ambassadors of metropolitan style.[15] This is not to suggest that feminine desires were uncatered for in the new retail landscape, but it is noteworthy that, while fashionable masculine dress was becoming increasingly associated with the British capital, Paris remained the centre for the production and dissemination of the leading modes for elite women. From the 1780s until 1815, however, successive trade embargoes and the hostilities of the Napoleonic wars kept British consumers at one remove from the novelties that Paris had to offer. Their reprieve allowed London traders, bolstered by the presence of French émigrés, including at one stage Marie Antoinette's former *marchande de modes* Rose Bertin, to establish themselves as primary outlets for the textiles and trimmings that contributed to the making of fashionable costumes, even if the inspiration for their design remained avowedly French in spirit. Princess Charlotte, daughter of the Prince Regent, was no great leader of fashion, but even she was able to dress with a degree of magnificence thanks to the attention of royal provisioners including the silk mercer William King of Pall Mall and the London dressmakers Mrs Triaud and Mrs Bean, who worked on her trousseau, (fig. 21). Furthermore, a contemporary description of the dress worn by Charlotte at the queen's

Fig. 22   'Messrs Harding Howell &
Co., 89, Pall Mall', *The Repository of
Arts, Literature, Commerce,
Manufactures, Fashions and Politics*,
March 1809. Published by Rudolph
Ackermann. Harding Howell &
Company's Grand Fashionable
Magazine at 89 Pall Mall had four
departments selling fur and fans; dress
fabrics, haberdashery, lace and acces-
sories; jewellery, fancy goods and per-
fume; millinery and dress.

drawing room in May 1815 gives no indication that British-made fashions were in any sense infe-
rior in construction or visual impact:

> Her dress on this occasion was exquisitely beautiful. Gold lama and white draperies over a
> petticoat of rich white satin; beneath the draperies a trimming of superb blond lace, headed
> with a wreath of white satin and gold twisted trimming; train of rich figured white satin, body
> elegantly trimmed with rich gold and blond lace; head-dress, plume of ostrich feathers, with
> a beautiful diadem of brilliants; necklace and ear-rings of diamonds.[16]

For less exalted, but reasonably well-off customers, the businesses of drapers, silk mercers
and haberdashers proliferated across the city, providing the basic components for garments
that would either be made up by a professional dressmaker or put together with the aid of servants at home. At this stage even hats were generally trimmed according to the individual taste
of the owner, following the purchase of a basic straw bonnet or a cloth base, rather than being
bought ready-finished. The choice of textiles available to the London consumer, generally
bought in seven-yard lengths (which in 1800 would produce one gown), was infinite, reflecting
the capital's power as a centre of international trade and commerce.[17] A visitor to the city at
the turn of the century was struck by the cosmopolitan nature of the drapers' stores in the
vicinity of Ludgate Hill, but such choice and opulence was common from the City to the West
End (fig. 22):

> The shops are perfect gilded theatres, the variety of wrought silks so many changes of fine
> scenes, and the mercers are the performers in the opera...They are the sweetest, fairest,
> nicest, dished-out creatures; and by their elegant address and soft speeches, you would guess
> them to be Italians. As people glance within their doors, they salute them with – 'Garden-
> silks, ladies; Italian silks; very fine mantua silks; any right Geneva velvet, English velvet, velvet
> embossed?' and to the meaner sort – 'Fine thread satins, both stripe and plain; fine mohair
> silks; satinets; burdets; Perianets; Norwich crapes; anterines; silks for hoods and scarves; hair
> camlets, druggets, sagathies; gentlemen's nightgowns ready-made, shalloons, durances, and
> right Scotch plaids.'[18]

MORNING DRESS.

In similar vein, Jane Austen patronised a series of retailers during her visits to London, betraying like many tourists her excitement at being able to engage with the latest 'trophy' products and rub shoulders with a multitude of fashionable shoppers. The key stops for her were the drapers Widing and Kent in Grafton House, New Bond Street; the mercers Layton and Shear's in Henrietta Street, Covent Garden; and hosiers Crook, Son and Besford's in Pall Mall. In 1813 she wrote to her sister from London:

> I hope you will receive the Gown tomorrow & may be able with tolerable honesty to say that you like the Colour; – it was bought at Grafton House, where, by going very early, we got immediate attendance, & went on very comfortably. – I only forgot the one particular thing which I had always resolved to buy there – a white silk Handkf – & was therefore obliged to give six shillings for one at Crook & Besford's . . . we must have been 3 qrs of an hour at Grafton House, Edward sitting by all the time with wonderful patience. There Fanny bought the Net for Anna's gown, and a beautiful Square veil for herself. – The Edging there is very cheap, I was tempted by some, & bought some very nice plaiting Lace at 3–4.[19]

London's reputation as a source of unusual goods was not restricted to the domestic consumer. Provincial retailers also travelled to the capital to stock up on fancy and cutting-edge items from the trade warehouses that were establishing themselves on the western edge of the City during this period. In the final decades of the eighteenth century, Elizabeth Towsey, a milliner and haberdasher of Chester, visited London at regular intervals to order new merchandise. On one occasion she left explicit instructions with her forewoman, Miss Legge, who was travelling down on her behalf, to call on a long list of traders and weigh up prices and quality:

In the first place call at Steward, Pavold and Smiths, where settle our accounts and look at

Fig. 23   Indian muslin dress, c.1805. Embroidered with a trailing leaf motif in chain stitch.

Fig. 24   'Afternoon Dresses', *The Gallery of Fashion*, February 1802. Hand coloured aquatint by published Nicolaus von Heideloff (1761–1837). The hair of the model on the left is dressed à l'antique. She is wearing a round dress of white embroidered muslin finished with a deep lace ruff. The figure on the right is wearing a black velvet hat à la Billington trimmed with ostrich feathers. Both figures carry swan's down muffs. The Harry Matthews Collection, Museum of London.

Fig. 25   'Morning Dress', *The Repository of Arts, Literature, Commerce, Manufactures, Fashions and Politics*, May 1812. Published by Rudolph Ackermann. This 'French frock of plain India muslin with a demi-train and long, full bishops' sleeves' is described as being the 'invention' of Mrs Gill of Cork Street, Burlington Gardens.

Fig. 26   *Panorama of Almack's Assembly Rooms, St James's, London,* 1819–20. Watercolour ascribed to Charlotte Augusta Sneyd (1800–82). The whole painting shows 154 identified figures (No. 75 is the Duke of Wellington) and measures 25.4 x 203.4cm. The Sneyd Papers, Keele University Library.

modes of all sorts, at the white silk, the blue and green. Do not buy any…Then go to Harris and Penny, pay their bill, and just look at what kind of fancy gloves they have to sell … You may then go to Bread Street. Just call in at Adams, and if they have any pretty fancy ribbons, pick out a few. Get the bill made out and take it with you to Drury's, which is just by there …And be sure to get some white souflee for tippets as we have some bespoke for next week.[20]

Personal visits were not the only means by which consumers and businesses apprised themselves of the latest metropolitan trends. A key London-based innovation of the early nineteenth century was the developed of the specialised fashion and lifestyle magazine that would so dominate fashion trends in the twentieth century. Growing out of the aristocratic society journals and scandal sheets that had emerged from the coffee-house culture of the late seventeenth century, illustrated guides to modes and manners aimed largely at genteel women readers also owed a debt to the sophisticated etiquette manuals, pocket books and almanacs with their lavishly engraved plates found in Paris before the Revolution, with competing sources also available in Weimar, Leipzig and Berlin. The isolation of Paris in the late 1780s and 90s contributed to the reorientation of fashion publishing across Europe and its further development in London. In London, émigré German publishing entrepreneurs Nicolaus von Heideloff and Rudolph Ackermann launched innovative and profitable titles including *The Gallery of Fashion* (1794) and *The Repository of Arts, Literature and Commerce* (1809). Both capitalised on Britain's growing sense of economic and industrial confidence.

Von Heideloff's *Gallery of Fashion* deliberately promoted the fashion choices and lifestyles of the British aristocracy. Its coloured plates depicted society hostesses clothed in neoclassical drapes, suggesting that London was the new Rome (fig. 24). *The Gallery of Fashion* echoed the educational impetus that lay behind design reformer Thomas Hope's publications: *Household Furniture and Decoration* (1807) and *Designs of Modern Costume* (1812). Hope's house in Duchess Street, which inspired the illustrations in *Household Furniture*, was a beacon of the new classical styles, and in his publishing ventures he ensured that the capital gained international recognition for its status as a generator of design ideas. Ackermann's *Repository* also took the innovative step of showing clothing alongside furniture and interiors (fig. 25). The resulting scenes were engraved to a high standard in the elegant spare lines promoted by London-based artists such as Flaxman and Fuseli. However, though cut off from its dictates, and in spite of the efforts of Hope and others, many Londoners continued to associate Paris with fashionability. In the same way that British dressmakers were prone to give themselves and their creations spurious French names, popular periodicals such as John Bell's *La Belle Assemblée* (1806) strove to retain a suggestion of Gallic sophistication, if only in the punning title. Yet in reality, Bell's journal relied on English artists and engravers for its illustrative content and was noteworthy for its rational organisation, rapport with readers of several classes and literary flair. In many ways it established an enduring format for the modern woman's magazine in its lively mix of social reportage, fashion, practical advice and the advertising of luxuries.[21]

Fig. 27   *The British Pugilist*, 1828. Marble sculpture by Charles Rossi (1762–1839). Petworth House, The Egremont Collection (The National Trust). Photograph: Photographic Survey, Courtauld Institute of Art.

HIGH AND LOW LIFE

Informed by a high level of style intelligence provided by the capital's burgeoning fashion press and dressed in the best products that the city's shops and warehouses could offer, the modish Londoner of *c*.1820 was presented with a panorama of possibilities within which to test the effectiveness of their newly fashionable, cosmopolitan identity. In many ways it was London society itself, its institutions and pursuits, that gained most recognition as a transformed and transforming leader of modern taste. As historian Peter Thorold has remarked, for men such as Chateaubriand, who experienced the delights of London as French Ambassador in 1822, the social whirl of the city set a series of unprecedented sartorial challenges :

> One never stopped changing clothes … He was up at six am for a breakfast party in the country – and back in London for lunch. He then changed his clothes for a walk in Bond Street or Hyde Park. After that he changed for seven thirty dinner. Then came the opera and another set of clothes, followed – changing again – by the evening assembly known as a 'rout'. What a life, he thought; the galleys would be a hundred times preferable.[22]

This sense of diversion, contrast and change, however taxing, lent Regency London its special character as an exciting fashion city relatively unconstrained by the tyrannies of official (that is royal) or religious deference. Bolstered by the power of money, the seeker after wealth, pleasure or status could use the constantly shifting, usually unwritten rules of deportment and etiquette to fulfil their goals. Such a quest could often see them range across social boundaries in a manner unthinkable in other European capitals. It was inevitable that something of this freedom would find its reflection in dress, even if, as for Chateaubriand, the incessant choices were exhausting.

The sites of fashionable life were as varied as the changes of clothes demanded by them. At the apex of the social pyramid in London were the assembly rooms: Almack's in King Street, St James's, the Argyll Rooms in Little Argyll Street and the New Assembly Rooms in Hanover Square. Purpose-built assembly rooms had developed across England from the 1720s as locations for banquets, dances and concerts. Designed to opulent standards, they generally contained a ballroom with musicians gallery, a card room for gambling and a refreshment room. Almack's, opened in 1764, was by far the most exclusive, and rapidly gained a reputation as an elite marriage market (fig. 26). Its customers gave themselves over to the pleasures of courtship while acknowledging the strict control of a cartel of aristocratic women who ran the club

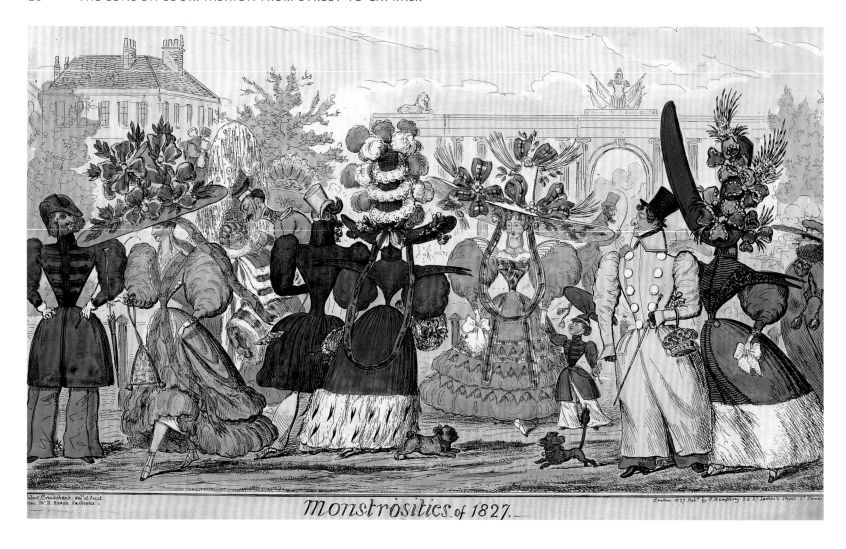

Monstrosities of 1827.

Fig. 28   *Monstrosities of 1827* 'after Mr. B. Reads fashions'. Drawing and engraving by Robert Cruikshank (1789–1856).

and determined who might enter.[23] Almack's infamous masquerades attracted huge crowds of revellers in outlandish fancy-dress costumes. Alongside the pleasure gardens and the opera house, such sites of genteel debauchery cemented London's notoriety as a city of conspicuous consumption and bold display.[24]

If the world of the assembly room was associated with aristocratic excess and a freer eroticism in women's dress, other leisure venues in London suggested the rather narcissistic, masculinist concerns of the dandy, or the rougher self-presentation of the sporting man. In these male arenas, the class divisions accentuated at Almack's dissolved in a deliberate mixing of high and low styles. Tattersall's, the horse dealer at Hyde Park Corner, was a typical haunt of the déclassé man about town. Pierce Egan described it as 'the most complete place in the metropolis' and recommended that 'if you have any desire to witness real life – to observe character – and to view the favourite hobbies of mankind', a visit was compulsory:

> It is the resort of the pinks of the swells, – the tulips of the goes, – the dashing heroes of the military, – the fox hunting clericals, – the sprigs of the nobility, – stylish coachmen, – smart guards, – saucy butchers, – natty grooms, – tidy helpers, – knowing horse dealers, – betting politicians, – neat jockeys, – sporting men of all descriptions, – and the picture is finished by numbers of real gentlemen. It is the tip-top sporting feature of London.[25]

Alongside the glamorous world of equestrian pursuits, which dictated the neat and functional, but always subtly flash, tailoring that underpinned developing notions of formal English fashion, Pierce Egan chronicled the concerns of the 'fancy'. These followers of the art of boxing lent their version of stylish dressing to the emergence of the London look. In his *Boxiana or Sketches of Ancient and Modern Pugilism*, Egan celebrated the cult of the prize-fighter (fig. 27) whose muscular pose was in many ways a mirror image of the self-regarding dandy's fashionable stance. In reference to the most popular club for supporters of the ring, he stated that 'it was ... for the purposes of the truest patriotism and national benefit that the Pugilistic Society was formed ... The great object of it is to keep alive the principles of courage and hardihood which have distinguished the British character, and to check the progress of that effeminacy which wealth is apt to produce.'[26] Members of the society could even adopt a uniform – a blue coat and yellow kerseymere waistcoat – which carried unintentional echoes of Beau Brummell's attire.

However, it was the fighter himself who offered the most compelling model for the new meritocratic art of London dressing. Egan noted that the impressive six-foot, fifteen-stone frame of retired boxer Bob Gregson was the focus for much admiration.

> A finer or better proportioned athletic man could not be met with ... He was considered by the celebrated professor of anatomy at the Royal Academy a most excellent subject to descant upon ... He was likewise selected by the late Sir Thomas Lawrence as a fine subject ... his general deportment was above all absurd affectation; nothing supercilious was to be found in his manner ... [he] was always well, nay fashionably dressed.'[27]

From 1810 Gregson managed The Tavern, a public house in Holborn much favoured by modish young men. His success was repeated in the founding of several sporting houses, many of them run by retired fighters, across the East End of London, from Smithfield to Moorgate to the Old Kent Road. That similar retreats could also be found in Fitzroy and Grosvenor Squares, in Bond Street and Jermyn Street, betrays the extent to which the fashionable character of London respected no social boundaries. As the satirist Bernard Blackmantle suggested in 1826, the city's vibrant fashion culture thrived on the clashing and complementary influences which were inevitable in a world metropolis now marked by its size, wealth and diversity:

> In Cockneyland, the seventh day
> Is famous for a grand display
> Of modes, of finery and dress
> Of Cit, West-Ender and Noblesse,
> Who in Hyde Park crowd like a fair
> To stare, and lounge and take the air,
> Or ride, or drive, or walk and chat
> On fashions, scandal and all that.[28]

Dress for the Theatres.

Newest Fashions for November 1831. Morning and Evening Dresses.

2 CLOTHING A WORLD CITY: 1830–60 *Edwina Ehrman*

When King George IV died in 1830, the public show of mourning in London was perfunctory. Few would have argued with the obituary that appeared in *The Times* attacking the king's 'reckless, unceasing and unbounded prodigality' that had strained the public purse and squeezed his creditors. Proof of his sartorial extravagance was amply provided by the sale of his clothing and personal effects that took place over three days in December 1830.[1] As dealers, souvenir and bargain hunters and the merely curious picked over the king's wardrobe, the tastes and weaknesses of a man who had been an acknowledged arbiter of style were laid bare. The luxurious fabrics and trimmings, richly decorated military coats, and above all his Highland outfits reflected his relish for pageantry and theatrical display.

The king was also highly attuned to the nuances of fashion (fig. 30). He was an informed and demanding client with a fastidious eye. The trousers, pantaloons and breeches, waistcoats, coats and greatcoats listed in lot after lot had all been made to his exacting standards by London's finest tailors who had an international reputation for expertise and taste. And it was not just the king and the West End elite who were so style-conscious. Fashion was a '*turn-coat whirligig maniac* . . . the idol of Paris and London, and the sun of the western hemisphere: in the metropolis it is this that entirely governs the dressing department, from the first-rate exquisite of the nobility, who has the last new superb cut from Stultz's, down to the shop-swell in the east, "vot has the last reg'lar *bang-up-go*" from the Borough'.[2]

READY-MADE TAILORING

In the 1830s the ready-made tailoring trade in London and the south of England expanded into juvenile clothing and fashionable menswear in the 1830s, offering stylish clothing at competitive prices and the opportunity for men to acquire larger wardrobes. For many, new clothes and the

Fig. 29 (*facing*)   'Dress for the Theatres, Newest Fashions for November, 1831. Morning and Evening Dresses', *World of Fashion*, November 1831.

Fig. 30 (*left*)   *The King*, 1821–30. Lithograph after Charles Hullmandel (1789–1850). This print shows George IV driving a phaeton.

self-respect they conferred became affordable for the first time. Before this, the trade had been concentrated in the production of standardised lines such as uniforms and servants' liveries, although some tailors and second-hand clothes dealers carried small stocks of ready-made clothing as a sideline. After the French wars, which ended with the Battle of Waterloo in 1815, the price of textiles fell, making new clothes accessible to more people and cutting into the second-hand market. At the same time, technological developments in textile manufacturing increased the range of woven fabrics in the middle price range, creating a greater variety of accessibly priced materials. These developments, coupled with the introduction of more sophisticated methods of pattern-cutting, encouraged a shift towards the production of more fashion-conscious clothing. Entrepreneurs who entered the trade based their business strategy on the principle of cash payments for fixed-price goods, with low margins and a high turnover. They also offered a money-back guarantee; the largest had the financial backing to take advantage of fluctuations in the market and to buy in bulk at advantageous prices, enabling them to pass on more savings to the consumer. They also invested heavily in advertising and in acquiring and fitting out premises in prime locations.

Two of the most successful London firms were Hyam & Company (fig. 31) and Elias Moses & Son.[3] Both families were originally second-hand clothes dealers with links to the ready-made tailoring trade. Moses was based in the East End but the Hyam family, who were also pawnbrokers, came from Colchester in Essex where they continued to commission clothing and, from the 1860s, to manufacture it in their own factory. Both firms established themselves in the City of London, which remained a key shopping centre for menswear, before opening West End branches. The City, as the financial and commercial hub of the country and the empire, was close

Fig. 31   Advertisement for L. Hyam's Pantechnetheca, c.1844.

Fig. 32   Advertisement for E. Moses & Son of Aldgate and the Minories in the City of London. In 1851, the year of the Great Exhibition, the firm opened a West End branch in Oxford Street.

to the docks, and was served by the General Post Office in St Martin-le-Grand, where goods could be dispatched all over the world, and the capital's developing railway system, which connected London with the leading provincial towns where the firms had branches and business interests. The scale of their operations was ambitious, integrating manufacturing, wholesaling and retailing, tailoring and outfitting, and the sale of ready-made and bespoke garments. They exported goods and, in the case of Moses, imported wool and hides from Australia, where both had branches. Their stock was split between standardised clothing and more fashionable wear. They supplied uniforms, servants' liveries, work wear, outfits for emigrants and mourning clothes, and offered a contract clothing service for the clergy, professionals and tradesmen, as well as a mail order service for self-measured bespoke. Both Moses and Hyam sold women's riding habits, which were traditionally made by tailors, and by 1851 Moses had expanded into furs, shawls, hosiery, footwear and parasols (fig. 32).

The industry relied on the ready availability of cheap labour. In 1846 Moses claimed to employ over 3,500 hands, but if Hyam is to be believed, his was the more substantial business.[4] In 1852 he numbered his workforce at over 8,000 people with a further 30,000 dependent on the firm.[5] Although Hyam condemned businesses where 'the price of labour is reduced to the lowest stipend', his stock, like many other tailors and clothiers, such as Samuel Brothers and H. J. & D. Nicoll, was made by the 'sweated system', where the manufacturing was contracted to a small master or 'sweater' who subcontracted the work to semi-skilled men and women working at home or in small workshops. The trade was unregulated and the workers, paid by the piece, earned no

Fig. 33 Silk satin waistcoat, 1850s. The quality of fabric and workmanship of this waistcoat embroidered with lilies of the valley suggest that it was custom-, not ready-made.

Fig. 34   Samuel Brothers produced a series of humorous and topical cards with fabric swatches attached advertising their 'Sydenham' trousers, c.1855.

more than subsistence wages for injuriously long hours. In the early 1840s Hyam attributed the low cost and alleged quality of his waistcoats to the subdivision of labour integral to 'sweating'. 'Each waistcoat having to pass through six different hands, it is but natural to suppose each would be perfect and doubly quick in their several departments; hence the great saving of labour and perfection of workmanship united, enables him to sell a Waistcoat complete in every respect, at a less price than a tailor would charge for the workmanship alone.'[6] Most off-the-peg clothes were made by hand until about 1860 when Greenwood & Batley's band knife – first envisioned by the Leeds tailor John Barran and able to cut through many layers of cloth – made the sewing machine more commercially viable.[7]

The abuses of the sweated system, which was common to most of the clothing trades, were exposed by the radical journalist Henry Mayhew and the satirical magazine *Punch*. A less well-known writer John Fisher Murray blamed bargain hunters, seduced by the boldly advertised discounts, for perpetuating the system:

> We have no patience with the hungry-eyed, greedy-hearted wretches who rush into cheap shops; the only respectability about the cheap shops is their cleverness in *doing* these hunters of bargains. It is not that the buyer is sure at these places to get an article fifty percent *worse*, at five and twenty percent *less* than a respectable tradesman can afford to sell it for; this we rejoice at; this is a sort of retributive justice; it serves the bargain-hunter right. It is the misery among tradespeople, artificers, shopmen, the *screwing* of the poor workmen and workwomen, to which the bargain-hunter, by his purchases, is an accessory after the fact, that makes the true ground of lamentation.[8]

The fashionable clothes advertised by Hyam, Moses and their competitors were made for men who wanted the clothing opportunities enjoyed by the higher social classes. The standard garments of coat, waistcoat, trousers and topcoat were available in a range of imaginatively named styles and a large choice of materials, at prices which reflected the variety of cut, fabrics and trimmings. Colourful, patterned 'fancy' waistcoats were particularly fashionable (fig. 33) and were available in materials such as satin, velvet plush and, for the extravagant or showy customer, bespoke in rich figured velvet. Seasonal advertisements were formulated to encourage the purchase of leisure wear, for a day out at the races or an excursion to the seaside, as well the appropriate sportswear for walking and the country pursuits of hunting, shooting and fishing. Moses and H. J. & D. Nicoll frequently advertised designs they had registered under the 1839 Design

Copyright Act, drawing attention to the novelty and originality of their stock, while Samuel Brothers promoted their own brand of 'Sydenham' trousers, which cost seventeen shillings and sixpence whether they were made-to-measure or ready-made (fig. 34). Samuel stressed the respectability and quality of their stock, guaranteeing to supply 'the following desideratum essential in a Gentleman's dress: – *First Quality of Cloth, Elegance, Style, Ease, a Good Fit, Gentlemanly Appearance*, and the greatest *Economy*, consistent with the *Best Workmanship and Materials*'.9

Each firm provided a bespoke service that implicitly enhanced their status, broadened their appeal and offered customers the opportunity of using it for garments like trousers which were more difficult to fit, in tandem with their ready-to-wear stock. Samuel offered customers the choice of being measured at their premises at Ludgate Hill or at home. Moses' bespoke clients had to visit his shop, but the department was entered through a private waiting hall which gave a gloss of exclusivity to the service. Many customers may have preferred the anonymity of the shop to exposing their home to the prying eyes of an unknown tailor. Moses' early promotions for his service were characteristically vainglorious and combative. His cutters were 'Artists of *undoubted talent and celebrity*', whose skills created garments with:

> all the essentials of superior style or *Haut Ton*, of elegance of Fit, and durability, and perfection of Workmanship, ... ensuring to the Nobility, Gentry, Tradesmen and Artizans, a Suit of Clothes suited to their wishes ... at ONE HALF THE PRICE they were charged before the opening of this establishment, and fully **Forty-five per Cent.** less than those Houses which have since pretended to do business (with specious promises) on their plan.10

Hardly any ready-made menswear from this period has survived, but the novelty and sheer quantity of advertising material, which ranged from boldly printed broadsheets and pages of doggerel verse in the 1840s to flyers, almanacs, magazines and brochures in next decade, has ensured the longevity of this ephemeral evidence of the trade (fig. 36).

THE GENT

I'm a gent – I'm a gent – I'm a gent ready made
I rove thro' the Quadrant and Lowther Arcade
I'm a register'd swell from the head to the toe
I wear a moustache and a light paletôt [11]

Fig. 36 (*above*)   Sheet music for the comic song 'I'm a Gent – I'm a Gent', *c*.1855. Spellman Collection of Victorian Music Covers, The University of Reading.

Fig. 35 (*left*)   Ready-made silk satin stock, 1840s. Retailed by Welch & Margetson, whose name is printed in copperplate script on the lining.

Fig. 37   Novelty cravat pins, 1850–70.

Fig. 38   Silver plated watch chain
with a horn-shaped trinket set with
a compass, 1860s.

The paletôt was a loose hip-length coat associated with H. J. & D. Nicoll, self-styled 'Patentees of the registered Paletôt' as their advertisements put it, whose extensive premises were adjacent to the Quadrant in Regent Street. As this ditty implies, 'gents', or 'swells' as they were also known, patronised the ready-made trade. They were not gentlemen but clerks working in government and commercial offices and warehouses, shop assistants, apprentices, hack journalists, medical students and the sons of respectable middle-class families. Albert Smith dissected their habits and appearance in *The Natural History of the Gent* published in 1847. He attributed their interest in fashion to their ambitions to be taken for gentlemen, but their singular style and laddish behaviour were more self-consciously alternative, appropriating rather than imitating the style and pleasures of the upper classes, marking them out as a group with their own subcultural identity. Their exaggerated clothes were either loose or very close fitting and accessorised with a shiny black silk top hat worn at a cocky angle, dainty boots and a fancy walking stick. They wore ready-made black silk stocks (fig. 35) of unusual designs or figured cravats stuck with novelty pins (fig. 37), with bright waistcoats and boldly patterned trousers. Shawls and printed silk handkerchiefs worn trailing from their coat pockets added more layers of fabric, colour and pattern, tantalising the city's pickpockets. Rings flashed on their slightly grubby gloved fingers, which concealed their neglected hands, and they played incessantly with the trinkets (fig. 38), purchased in the Lowther Arcade, suspended from their heavy watch chains. Their luxuriant hair was dressed with musk and patchouli oil and their clothes reeked of cigars. They were flashy spenders as well as flashy dressers, and they caroused in boisterous gangs in song and supper rooms like the Cyder Cellars and Evans in Covent Garden where the largely male audience was entertained with glees, comic songs and blue jokes. They met in cigar divans, where pornography was peddled in the less reputable dives and billiard halls. On summer evenings, they donned evening dress and took cabs to Cremorne Gardens in Chelsea, where they drank champagne and mingled with the *demi-mondaines* who clustered around the gas-lit dancing platform (fig. 39).

In the masculine environment of the City, the majority of men who thronged the streets dressed unremarkably. But alternative styles thrived, particularly among the young, who dramatised their lifestyles and expressed their group identity in unorthodox or exaggerated styles of dress. 'Many of the young stock and produce brokers display great anxiety to be peculiar in their dress, which occasions a rage every now and then among them for strangely-fashioned hats, deep striped shirts, long-waisted coats, and other articles of clothing, which attract the eye and make a sensation.'[12] Stockbrokers were also known as sporting men. These 'City dandies', 'shining with

new clothes and jewellery', drove into the City in dog-carts and were habitués of Tattersall's.[13] Other young City workers, who commuted by coach from the suburbs, affected the dress of coachmen, wearing white topcoats decorated with large pearl buttons, while men working in the London Commercial Salerooms wore low crowned hats and 'trousers of strange patterns'.

The junior clerks in the 'flash' houses followed the gents' fashions fed to them by the ready-made trade.

> These are the dashing young parties who purchase ... the crimson braces, the kaleidoscopic shirt-studs, the shirts embroidered with dahlias, deaths' heads, race-horses, sun-flowers, and ballet-girls ... These are the glasses of city fashion, and the mould of city form, for whom the legions of fourteen, of fifteen, of sixteen and of seventeen shilling trousers, all unrivalled, patented, and warranted, are made; for these ingenious youths coats with strange names are devised; scarves and shawls of wondrous pattern and texture despatched from distant Manchester and Paisley ... [14]

Brokers could earn £60 or £70 a year rising to £300, and clerks from £50 up to £250 for a ledger clerk.[15] These dress-conscious young men spent freely on their appearance, responding enthusiastically to the novelties devised by manufacturers like John Edward Ford of Addle Street, who registered a design for a floral embroidered shirt in 1846, and Richard Ford, who sold printed and aniline dyed shirts in his shop in the Poultry. [16]

Womenswear manufacturers did not start to explore the full potential of ready-to-wear until the 1870s. Until then most women's ready-made garments were loose and semi-fitted. Thomas Ford offered women's mantles, jackets, blouses and riding habits at his premises at 42 Oxford

Fig. 39   *The Dancing Platform at Cremorne Gardens*, 1864. Oil painting by Phoebus Levin (fl. 1855–78).

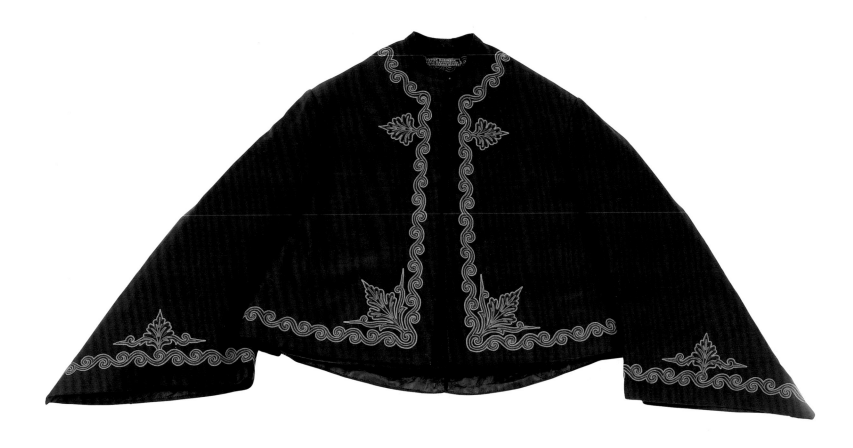

Street. In 1861 his stock included a number of fashionable embroidered Zouave jackets, inspired by the uniforms worn by the French Zouave regiments in the Crimean War.[17] Mail-order customers were asked to send their measurements or, if they wished to purchase a tight-fitting jacket, an existing bodice, suggesting that the garments were partly or wholly made to order. Peter Robinson – who by 1860 had transformed his single drapery outlet into one of the largest department stores in Oxford Street – sold millinery, made-to-measure outfits and mourning clothes alongside loose-fitting ready-made garments, such as mantles and 'flounced silk skirts, plain or trimmed with velvet'.[18] A black wool Zouave jacket, in the collection of the Museum of London, was retailed by Peter Robinson around 1863. Embroidered in chain stitch with pink silks in an arabesque pattern, it carries the firm's earliest label (fig. 40).[19] Although shoemakers and hatters had used labels since the late eighteenth century, women's clothing retailers did not introduce them to encourage consumer loyalty until the 1860s. Alongside Marshall & Snelgrove – which by 1866 occupied an island site with entrances on Oxford Street, Vere Street and Henrietta Street and sold a huge range of women's clothing and accessories as well as fancy goods, household linen and furnishings – department stores such as Peter Robinson were gradually turning the mixed commerce of Oxford Street into the mainstream clothing store byword it is today.

FASHION INFORMATION

The emphasis on fit and fashion in early nineteenth-century tailoring led to the publication of a string of technical tailoring books which promoted the pattern-cutting systems devised by their authors. It also led to the first fashion publication dedicated to menswear. Several enterprising tailor authors, of whom the best known is Benjamin Read, also published large hand-coloured aquatints of the latest fashions which were marketed as a guide for tailors. Read's prints, issued twice a year, were sold with patterns and information for between seven and ten shillings.[20] The foreground of each plate contains about ten boldly drawn figures of men, women and boys whose mannered poses and fastidious gestures are frozen in a surreal state of suspended anima-

Fig. 40 a and b   Zouave jacket sold by Peter Robinson of Oxford Street, c.1863.

tion. The doll-like figures are positioned to show the costumes from a range of angles, giving the tailor and his customer an overview of the cut and style of each garment. The prints date from the mid-1820s to 1848 and are set in a variety of fashionable locations from the royal parks and Oxford Street shopping bazaars (fig. 41) to popular places of entertainment like the Zoological Gardens and Madame Tussaud's Wax Works. Using topical London sites as backdrops for fashion plates was not new, but their social cachet and newsworthiness added value to the fashions. It also made the prints more eye-catching. Read exhibited them at the Royal Exchange and, if Albert Smith is to be believed, some tailors displayed them in their windows. [21] Ironically, the series may have been inspired by the 'Monstrosities' drawn by the artist George Cruikshank and issued annually from 1816 as parodies of the dandified dress and pretentious, vulgar manners of the London crowd as they paraded around Hyde Park. Read employed George's brother Robert to draw his plates until about 1830, and one can only speculate whether he took Robert's own 1827 'Monstrosities' print drawn 'from Mr. B. Reads fashions' (fig. 28) as a good joke and clever advertising stunt or as an insult.

Benjamin Read was also involved with *The Gentleman's Magazine of Fashions*, contributing to it from June 1840. The magazine's original title was *The Gentleman's Magazine of Fashions, Fancy Costumes and the Regimentals of the Army*. It was published by John Browne Bell of 3 Cleveland Row until 1850, with the earliest fashion information supplied by English, German and French tailors 'of the first eminence'. The frontispiece of the first issue in May 1828 depicted George IV. The tribute to the king was appropriate. Although by then a recluse, troubled by obesity and ill health, he had been one of the best dressed men of his generation and exemplified the expensive, immaculate, and understated elegance of the Regency dandy. The colourful, romantic and affected styles of the 1830s were very different, but as a thoroughly metropolitan man, the king would have agreed with the editorial stance of the first issue: 'We are not like *Frankenstein* about

Fig. 41   *A View in the Pantheon, London. Winter Fashions from Novr. 1834 to April 1835.* Published by Benjamin Read. The Pantheon in Oxford Street was converted into a shopping bazaar in 1834. Read's aquatint shows the upper gallery. Guildhall Library, Corporation of London.

Fig. 42   Beaver felt riding hat with a lace veil, *c.*1864. Retailed by W. C.Taylor and worn with the riding habit in fig. 43.

Fig. 43   Jacket of a woman's riding habit, *c.*1864. Tailored by W. C. Taylor, habitmaker, 53 Baker Street, London. The jacket is made of wool cloth and lined with silk. The bust has been lightly padded. Boning under the bust and beneath the centre front fastenings provides support and enhances the fit. The jacket was worn with a skirt which concealed trousers made from chamois leather (over the lower torso and thighs) and matching blue cloth.

to *make a man*; but we do intend to show the great world how a person of *ton* ought *to be dressed*; . . . inasmuch as he who is not from "head to foot, from top to toe" apparelled *à la mode*, is to all intents and purposes a *nobody*'![22] The publication had circulation problems and after four years it was reduced from twenty pages to four, with two rather than three plates. The text, which was directed at the trade, provided detailed descriptions of the cut of the latest fashions, including precise measurements for trousers, with information on colour, fabrics, trimmings and fastenings. The magazine also showed that, although London had a reputation for leading the field in menswear, fashion trends crossed the Channel in both directions. In January 1835 for instance, a double-breasted frock coat was featured with a sewn-on lapel which the Parisian tailor Straub claimed to have invented to improve the lie of the lapel.[23] Many London tailors came from across Europe and trained in their native countries before moving to the capital.

Bell also published a popular woman's magazine between 1824 and 1851. *World of Fashion and Continental Feuilletons* was 'Expressly dedicated to High Life, Fashionables and Fashions, Polite Literature, Fine Arts, the Opera, Theatres &c' (fig. 29). The magazine had distributors in England, Edinburgh, Dublin, Paris and New York and could be shipped to the 'East and West Indies'.[24] The fashion coverage was biased towards Paris with the commentary on the London modes peppered with French styles and novelties. Most of the fashion plates were engraved after French originals but a couple in 1831 incorporated images of society celebrities including the Countess of Jersey, whose husband had bred three Derby winners, and the Marchioness of Londonderry, who had dazzled the court with her astonishing array of jewellery at the recent coronation of William IV. From 1831, Mrs Bell designed and selected the fashions. This coincided with the removal of her dressmaking and millinery business to Mr. Bell's business address, conveniently situated opposite St James's Palace. The precise relationship between the Bells is not known, but their businesses were mutually profitable. Mrs. Bell, who was also a corsetière, employed French, German and Spanish milliners and claimed to import goods from Paris twice a week.

Townsend's Selection of Parisian Costumes, published for the trade between 1823 and 1888, was also illustrated with plates from Paris. London wholesale houses, tailors and dressmakers used the journal to promote their products in the provinces and advertise for apprentices and staff. The use of French fashion plates by magazines like *Townsend's* and the widely read *Englishwoman's Domestic Magazine* (1842–77), together with the sale of English-language versions of French fashion periodicals such as *Le Follet* (1829–92), reinforced France's dominance over women's fashions.

COQUETTES AND QUEENS

In the late afternoon, Rotten Row in Hyde Park was one of the sights of London:

> The Danaës! The Amazons! the lady cavaliers! the horsewomen! . . . Watch the sylphides as they fly or float past in their ravishing riding-habits and intoxicatingly delightful hats: some with the orthodox cylindrical beaver, with the flowing veil; others with roguish little wide-awakes, or pertly cocked cavaliers' hats and green plumes . . . from time to time the naughty wind will flutter the skirt of a habit, and display a tiny, coquettish, brilliant little boot, with a military heel, and tightly strapped over it the Amazonian riding trouser.[25]

Among the many respectable riders whose trim boots and spirited control of their mounts titillated the appreciative crowd of men gathered in the park were a number of well-known courtesans whose skilful horsemanship led to them being dubbed 'the pretty horsebreakers'. Queen of the horsebreakers was Skittles, or Catherine Walters, who was rumoured to wear nothing beneath her close-fitting riding habit, which was expertly tailored by Henry Poole of Savile Row. She was the mistress of the Marquis of Hartington from 1859 until 1863. It is thought that the couple met in Hyde Park where she showed off the paces of horses which were, like her, for sale.[26] The witty, beautiful but consumptive Annie Gilbert also rode in Rotten Row. She was the model for Edwin Landseer's painting *The Shrew Tamed, or the Pretty Horsebreaker* (1861) and for the woman in the riding habit in William Powell Frith's *Derby Day* (1858) where her position in the painting, opposite the roué, suggests an intimacy between them. Jacob Bell, who owned Tattersall's, introduced Gilbert and many of the other female models in the painting to Frith.[27]

Fig. 44   Detail of the fabric of a dress traditionally believed to have been worn by Queen Victoria during her state visit to Paris in August 1855. The watered, chiné silk was probably manufactured in France.

The ambivalence of the riding habit, which incorporated masculine style details and construction techniques in a garment that both showed off and concealed the female form, added to its allure for both sexes. A bespoke habit would be cut, moulded and padded to conform to the client's specifications and discreetly conceal any physical imperfections (fig. 43). The finished garment was sculpted to the body, but allowed complete freedom of movement. Max Schlesinger, visiting London from Germany in 1851, was surprised to see Queen Victoria and Prince Albert riding with little pomp through the crowd in the park.[28] The queen enjoyed riding and her finely tailored London-made habits flattered her figure. She appointed Peter Thompson of Frith Street in Soho as her habit maker in 1837, but from 1859 she patronised Henry Creed of Creed & Cumberland in Conduit Street.[29] The queen recommended him to the Empress Eugénie, wife of

Napoleon III, and Creed subsequently opened a branch in Paris specialising in English women's tailoring.[30] In the 1860s another Englishman, Charles Frederick Worth, became the empress's principal dressmaker. After serving an apprenticeship, possibly to Swan & Edgar, Worth had worked for the prestigious silk-mercers Lewis & Allenby before moving to Paris in 1846 to develop his career. Worth's commercial acumen in creating 'models' which could be distributed throughout the world, combined with the advantage of speaking English in a city where America was a growing market, laid the foundations of his highly profitable business.[31]

Queen Victoria was interested in fashion and admired the Empress Eugénie's stylish and elegant appearance. During the visit of the emperor and empress to London in 1855 and the British royal family's reciprocal visit to Paris, the queen meticulously recorded in her journal the clothes and jewels she and the empress had worn. Both women had magnificent collections of jewellery, but the queen's had been recently enriched by the East India Company's gift of the jewels from the treasury of Lahore taken by the British following their annexation of the Punjab in 1849. These included the legendary Koh-i-noor diamond, worn by the queen during the visit as a potent symbol of imperial wealth. The queen singled out Eugénie's appearance on the night before her departure: 'The Empress looked particularly lovely in a white net dress *à deux jupes*, trimmed with scarlet velvet bows and bunches of white lilacs, and two bows of the same, and diamond flowers in her hair. She looked so simple and elegant … I wore a blue dress, richly trimmed with lace, my rubies, and two feathers in my hair'.[32] Several of the queen's dresses had been specially purchased from the Parisian firms Palmyre & Legrand and Deschamps &

Sellier for the visit (fig. 44). Her aunt, Queen Louise of Belgium, had introduced her to the delights of Mlle Palmyre when she was sixteen and she had patronised the house ever since.

Although Queen Victoria recognised her responsibility to support the British and Irish textile industries by wearing their manufactures on state and public occasions and by sponsoring charitable events like the Plantagenet and Spitalfields balls in 1842, she had no inhibitions about wearing French luxury goods. The queen was not a leader of fashion, but the royal family attracted a great deal of public interest and her influence should not be underestimated. In London she patronised Mary Bettans in Jermyn Street from 1824 until 1844, and in the 1850s Elizabeth Gieve in Davies Street and Sarah Ann Unitt in Lower Grosvenor Street. She also favoured a number of houses run by French dressmakers resident in the capital: Vouillon & Laure in Princes Street, and Elise Papon and Papon & Phillippe in Grosvenor Street.[33] London's elite dressmaking houses continued to be located south and west of Hanover Square until the mid-twentieth century.

THE GREAT EXHIBITION

On 1 May 1851 Queen Victoria opened the Great Exhibition of the Works of Industry of All Nations in Hyde Park. The displays drawn from across the world were presented as a vehicle for peace, international cooperation and industrial progress. The organisers also hoped to prompt improvements in the manufacture and design of British goods, educate public taste and benefit

Fig. 45   Man's tartan silk velvet waistcoat, c.1850.

Fig. 46   British-made wool turnover shawl, c.1850. Hand-embroidered with floss silk in an Indian-style cone design. The popularity of Indian shawls encouraged British manufacturers to copy and adapt their patterns. The shawl was worn folded diagonally to show the two corner ornaments.

British trade. Although the exhibition did not overtly promote free trade, which remained a controversial issue, many of its supporters (including the queen and Prince Albert, who played a key role in the realisation of the exhibition) believed in its political and economic value. Over 100,000 objects were displayed in the Crystal Palace whose revolutionary design reflected the overall emphasis of the exhibition on progress and invention. A number of London firms exhibited fabrics and clothing. Lewis & Allenby showed a complex Jacquard-woven silk brocade; it incorporated fifteen colours, was designed by S. W. Lewis and woven in Spitalfields using almost 30,000 cards and 100 shuttles. Redmayne & Company of New Bond Street also exhibited an elaborate silk of their own design. In spite of these attempts to address design, it was generally agreed that the French silks were superior; once again France dominated the luxury fashion trades.

Queen Victoria's well-publicised visits to the Scottish Highlands and the purchase of Balmoral Castle in 1848 had rekindled the vogue for tartans created a quarter of a century before by the enormous success of Walter Scott's Waverley novels (fig. 45). The displays at the Great Exhibition reflected the Scottish fad. Isaac Boyd, a designer and silk manufacturer in Spital Square, showed a watered-silk dress fabric patterned with thistles, bells and heather. James Locke of Regent Street, one of a number of exhibitors specialising in Scottish goods, exhibited tartan shawls, men's mauds (shepherd's plaids popularly worn as wraps) and Scottish tweeds. Scottish manufacturers reacted swiftly to the craze, developing new tartans, checks and tweeds to satisfy the demand at home and abroad.

Underwear and fashionable accessories such as shawls (fig. 46) and bonnets dominated the British clothing displays. Several exhibitors showed registered and patented garments or multi-purpose clothing designed in the spirit of economy and invention. These included S. Powell's *bisunique* or reversible garments and William Cutler's *duplexa* morning and evening coat. The judges regretted the lack of interest from the bespoke and ready-made tailoring trade which employed 'so many thousands of hands', but the truth was that their shops were all the exhibition they needed.

GLASS AND GASLIGHT

Amid the distractions of the urban environment, fashion had to perform as place as much as attire. Moses' West End branch in New Oxford Street was a palace of mirrors and light. The entrance hall was clad with sheets of reflecting glass, appearing grander, lighter and more spacious than it really was and drawing the attention of the customer to his appearance. In the showroom, the ceiling was also mirrored, intensifying the sense of self and transforming the act of purchase into a performance.[34] At night the shop became a giant advertisement, illuminated by a dazzling display of gaslight, which glorified the conspicuous consumption of which it – as much as the gin palaces and music halls it anticipated – was a product.

London's exclusive shawl shops offered the carriage trade an equally theatrical experience. Their look was that of an oriental bazaar in a far-flung corner of the empire:

> These are more like the interior of a Sultan's divan than an English tradesman's shop; draperied and festooned as they now are with the rich productions of the looms of Thibet, Angola [*sic*], Cashmere, of more than Tyrian splendour of dye, and of patterns varied, it would seem to infinity. Rich carpets conceal the floors of these establishments, vases of rare and costly china are dispersed about the room … lustres of brilliant crystal depend from painted ceilings, and rosewood *tables* (here you see no vulgar counters) dispersed throughout the vast apartment are heaped with costly velvets, and piles of cloth of gold.[35]

Like Moses, the shawl shops Everington on Ludgate Hill and James Holmes & Company in Regent Street had both installed floor-to-ceiling mirrors and gas chandeliers. For most commentators, the high value and rarity of their goods justified these opulent and extravagant surroundings. Their proprietors were praised for their refinement, while Moses (the Jew) was vilified for his profligacy and presumption.[36]

Between these two extremes sat the experiences of most consumers. Jane Welsh Carlyle probably spoke for many middle-class women when her need for an everyday item of clothing revealed the difficulties of negotiating the new and old sartorial practices:

> I needed a little jacket for home wear, and, possessing a superfluous black silk scarf, I resolved, in a moment of economical enthusiasm, to make … a jacket out of it. For in spite of the 'thirty thousand distressed needlewomen' one hears so much of, the fact remains that nobody can get a *decent* article of dress made here, unless at enormous cost. And besides, the dressmakers who can fit one won't condescend to make anything but with their own materials. So I fell to cutting out that jacket last Monday, and only finished it today (Friday)! … But Lord preserve me, what a bother; better to have bought one ready-made at the dearest rate. I won't take a needle in my hands, except to sew on Mr. C.'s buttons, for the next six months.[37]

3   FASHION IN THE AGE OF IMPERIALISM: 1860–90   *Christopher Breward*

Nothing can be more prosaic or suggestive of the London struggle than a penny boat ... The keen newsboys, the negro minstrels, the lavender girls in the spring, the little vendors of cigar lights ... the women laden with bundles and children ... the boy-men bound on legal errands ... premature smokers, and ostentatious wearers of flowers, cravats and jewellery; the crisp, clean crowds of businessmen ... the lawyers with their blue bags ... the shop-girls and bar-maids of ample chignon and prodigal of colour, whom the clerks regard with tender glances ... An English crowd is almost the ugliest in the world: because the poorer classes are but copyists in costume, of the rich. The exceptions are the followers of street trades – the costermongers, the orange-women, and the tramps. The workman approximates his nearest cut to the cut of Poole. The English carpenter wears a black tail coat – like the waiter, the undertaker, and the duke. Poor English women are ghastly in their patches trimmed in out-landish imitation of the fashion. Le Follet's plans penetrate to Shoreditch: and the hoop, the chignon, and the bonnet no larger than a d'Oyley, are to be seen in Drury Lane and behind apple stalls. In these base and shabby copyings of the rich, the poverty of the wearers has a startling, abject air. It is, as I heard a stranger remark, 'misery advertised'.[1]

'Misery advertised' was indeed a striking description for the appearance of London and its popu-lation in 1872, the year in which the English journalist Blanchard Jerrold and his friend the French artist Gustave Doré published their classic tour of the high Victorian city, *London: A Pilgrimage* (fig. 48). This account of the shocking contrasts and alienating crowds of the capital provided a vivid graphic guide to the hellish terrain previously staked out by Henry Mayhew and Charles Dickens and set the context for the later urban critiques of George Gissing and Charles Booth.[2] It is undoubtedly a bleak vision that offers little succour to the fashion historian seeking any sense of the glamour or beauty generally understood to attend the history of dress. The Londoners depicted here, on board a Thames commuter boat, are unapologetic in their ugliness. Begrimed, lacking taste or originality, their clothing is a wretched demonstration of social decline, a snub to those standards of elegance which had marked out the metropolis for interna-tional praise only half a century before.

Look again, though, and there is evidence here of the rude variety: the self-confidence and jingo-istic pride that underpinned London's rise to prominence in the second half of the nineteenth century. London had become the hub of the most powerful empire in the world. While many con-temporary commentators on art, fashion and culture condemned the apparent viciousness and vulgarity of life across all levels of London society in this period, seeking selective respite in the gentler tastes of a mythologised past, other more pragmatic souls recognised that in its sartorial habits at least, the British capital offered a vital template for living in this most urban of contexts. A popular tourist guide of 1877 offered the statistical evidence to support such claims:

There are about 8,000 streets, lanes, rows &c., in the metropolis. From Charing Cross, within a six miles radius, there are something over 2,800 miles of streets. As regards trades generally, it is hard even to get anything like an approximate notion of their numbers ... But to specify a few, there are, say, about 130,000 shopkeepers, or owners of commercial establishments, who carry on more than 2,500 different trades ... Among ... these are, without counting purely

Fig. 48 (*above*)   'Ludgate Hill – A Block in the Street', *London: A Pilgrimage*, 1872. Blanchard Jerrold (1826–84). Wood engraving after Gustave Doré (1832–83).

Fig. 47 (*facing*)   Silk handkerchief, 1875–85. Printed in black ink from an engraved plate, with dyed border and watercolours added by hand.

Fig. 49   'The Haunted Lady, or "The Ghost" in the Looking Glass', *Punch*, 4 July 1863. Drawing by John Leech (1817–64).

PUNCH, OR THE LONDON CHARIVARI.—July 4, 1863.

THE HAUNTED LADY, OR "THE GHOST" IN THE LOOKING-GLASS.

MADAME LA MODISTE. "WE WOULD NOT HAVE DISAPPOINTED YOUR LADYSHIP, AT ANY SACRIFICE, AND THE ROBE IS FINISHED *À MERVEILLE*."

wholesale dealers … 2,755 tailors, (not including about 500 old clothesmen, wardrobe dealers, &c.,) about 3,347 bootmakers, about 450 hatters, and so forth. All these are master tradesmen or shopkeepers, irrespective of workmen, foremen, shopmen, clerks, porters, apprentices and families.[3]

Such figures are probably conservative estimates, for in the census of 1851 it had been computed that the clothing industries alone employed 28,000 men and 84,000 women. But what is clear is that the city's unprecedented wealth and size supported an army of workers whose labour for both local and colonial markets was devoted to the manufacture of dress items in all their forms. The extraordinary volume of material that passed through the hands of London's tailors, seamstresses and shop staff produced a sartorial language marked by its very excess and diversity. In the fields of clothing production, fashion retail, design innovation and the wearing of dress itself, the outcomes were arguably as important as anything coming out of Paris in the same period, and equally distinctive in terms of quality and appearance.

A Manufactory of Fashion

The production of clothing was spread across the physical and social terrain of London in the 1860s and 70s. In Marylebone and Westminster, dressmakers and bespoke tailors sewed high-quality goods for the rich; skilled leather workers, straw plaiters and felters constructed shoes and hats in Bermondsey, Hackney and Southwark; silk weavers still operated their looms in Bethnal Green and Whitechapel – though trimmings such as ribbons had largely superseded the flowered dress and waistcoat silks of the previous century; while in neighbouring Stepney and Bow the sweated labour of women, children and recent immigrants (paid by the piece rather than the hour) produced cheap ready-made garments for working-class consumers.

These specialised centres of production, often relying on well-established systems of home-working and small workshops, were the key to the economic success of the London clothing trades at this time.[4] The ready supply of raw materials, workers, financial backing and buyers, together with the good communication and transport systems of the capital and a prohibitive lack of free or affordable space on which to build new industrial units, in effect slowed down the drift towards the large-scale, single-site mass-production systems (the monolithic mills and factories) that characterised cloth and garment manufacture in the north of England. London's rag-trade entrepreneurs could maintain an advantageous flexibility that responded well to shifts in taste – for their factory was the city itself. As one historian of the metropolis has remarked: 'in essence the [Victorian] city comprised ... a series of inter-related markets providing for the requirements of producers and consumers, lenders and borrowers, experts and inexperts – a national and international clearing house for goods, finance and expertise.'[5]

Though on the surface this system appeared to operate with fearsome efficiency, its powerful impetus was gained at the expense of a great deal of human happiness and comfort. In the summer of 1863, *Punch* magazine published a cartoon by John Leech entitled 'The Haunted Lady, or "The Ghost" in the Looking-Glass' (fig. 49). In it a fashionable lady turns to admire her new gown in her looking-glass. Shockingly, she is greeted by a reflection that includes the cadaverous spectre of an exhausted seamstress, whose demise has presumably been accelerated by the labour expended on the item the lady is trying on. 'We would not have disappointed your ladyship, at any sacrifice,' soothes her cynical dressmaker. 'And the robe is finished *a merveille*.' Leech was illustrating an article about a celebrated scandal which had rocked the West End in June 1863. An anonymous worker had written to *The Times* exposing the lethal conditions that existed in the workrooms of one Madame Elise of Regent Street, especially at busy times during the Season when demand for new items was intense. At other quieter times of the year, garment workers suffered the opposite effects of unemployment. The letter's direct and plaintive words were highly effective, at least in generating some temporary publicity for the plight of needlewomen in London's fashion industries:

> Sir, I am a dressmaker, living in a large West-end house of business. I work in a crowded room with 23 others. This morning one of my companions was found dead in her bed, and we all of us think that long hours and close confinement have had a great deal to do with her end. We are called in the morning at half-past 6, and in ordinary times we work until 11 at night, but occasionally our hours are much longer; on the Friday before the last Drawing Room, we worked all night, and did not leave off until 9 o'clock on Saturday morning.
>
> At night we retire to rest in a room divided into little cells, each just large enough to contain two beds. There are two of us in each bed. There is no ventilation; I could scarcely breathe in them when I first came from the country. The doctor who came this morning said they were not fit for dogs to sleep in.
>
> This poor girl was taken ill on Friday. We are often ill, so that not much notice is taken of that; she was worse on Sunday. Some of us sat up with her until she went to sleep. In the morning her bedfellow found her dead by her side.
>
> Of course we are all very much shocked, and although we do not complain of our house, which is better conducted than many, we should be so glad if some plan could be discovered by which we could get a little less work and a little more air.
>
> I remain, Sir,
> A Tired Dressmaker.[6]

The letter, together with the public inquest into the death of its unfortunate subject Mary Anne Walkley, generated a great deal of correspondence and editorial in the national press and in the pioneering woman's journal, *The Englishwoman's Domestic Magazine*. Questions were raised in both houses of parliament and official inspections of the West End fashion trades resulted, but with little tangible effect. The Isaacsons, who owned the Madame Elise business, weathered the storm. By 1870 they were listed in the London Directory as 'court dressmaker, milliner, silk manufacturer, antique and modern lace warehouse, and ladies outfitter, by special appointment dressmaker to H.R.H. the Princess of Wales' (fig. 50). What the scandal laid bare – and Leech's cartoon drew attention to – was the hypocrisy that allowed the system to flourish. As fashion historian

Fig. 50 a and b   Day dress, c.1875. Made by Madame Elise of Regent Street of silk trimmed with pleated tarlatan and three different patterns of black machine-made lace.

Christina Walkley notes: 'Isaacson was no more guilty of [Mary Anne Walkley's] death than any of his clients who demanded dresses or bonnets at short notice, than any of their husbands who expected them to dress showily at as little expense as possible, or than any of the thousands who believed that the working class, and especially the female working class, should accept their lot with patience and resignation.'[7]

Conditions in the elite menswear industries appeared to be a little less oppressive, for tailoring was still regarded as one of the most honourable of trade callings. During the 1860s, quintessential London businesses such as that of Henry Poole on Savile Row flourished without any of the negative publicity that dogged outfits like Madame Elise. Poole arrived on Savile Row in 1848, having built up an impressive list of royal and aristocratic customers from home and abroad since

Fig. 51   The jobbing tailor, *The British Workman*, c. 1860

Fig. 52   The exterior of Henry Poole illuminated for the state visit of the Emperor Louis Napoleon III of France, 1855. (Courtesy of Henry Poole & Company)

the firm's establishment in London in 1806. Poole's came to dominate the world of male fashion during the second half of the nineteenth century (fig. 52). Dandified clients such as Charles Dickens, Benjamin Disraeli and Edward, Prince of Wales acted as sartorial ambassadors for a subtle 'gentlemanly' style of dressing closely associated with London. Despite its veneer of respectability, Poole's calling was not entirely free of the stain of sweating, and tailors also endured the insecurity of seasonal employment and poor working environments. In 1888 the House of Lords instigated a series of committee hearings to investigate exploitative practices in the tailoring industries. Workshops in Soho and the East End were shown to be as grim as any in the millinery business, with workers completing eighteen hour days at starvation wages in crowded rooms with no sanitation, ventilation or light (fig. 51). The situation was heightened by the arrival of over 20,000 Jewish immigrants in London between 1880 and 1886 alone, many of them seeking work in the clothing trades.

Such conditions were more prevalent in those sectors dealing with ready-made rather than bespoke clothing. By the 1880s the London clothing industries had become more polarised in terms of their location and standards, between the rough rag-trade connotations of the East End and the fine craftsmanship and stable businesses associated with the West End. In the bespoke tailoring trades, the long apprenticeship and high levels of skill required, together with the patriarchal concern for employees typical of Savile Row's family firms, seemed to ward off the worst excesses of sweating. Poole's workshop in King Street (now Kingly Street) in Soho was set up in 1859, at a discreet remove from his customers in the Savile Row showroom. It was rebuilt in 1870 following a fire and represented a model of good employment practice for the time. The company historian cites an article on Poole's in the 1892 *London Art Fashion Journal* which aimed to 'place before the trade some ideas concerning the arrangement of the better class of workshops'. He continues:

The King Street workrooms were spread over three floors, of which the topmost was considered the healthiest: unlike the others it had no coke burning stove and there were ventilators in the roof ... [The] premises overall employed about seventy journeymen and regulars, of whom up to twenty-four worked in the top room, seated on the floor, starting at 6 a.m. and going through until 7 p.m., 'except in the summer time, when we often worked until it was

Fig. 53   'Two o'clock p.m.: Regent Street', *Twice Around the Clock*, 1859. George Augustus Sala (1828–96). Engraving after William M'Connell (d. 1867).

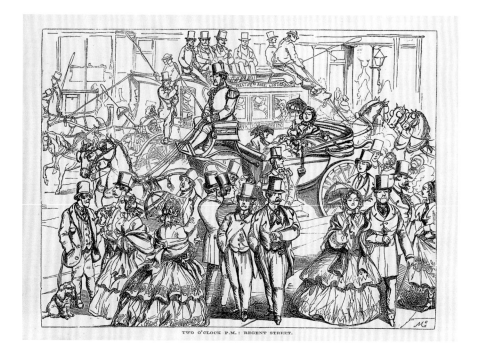

dark.' There was generally a plentiful supply of garments to work on; two porters or 'trotters' swept out the rooms in turns; a timekeeper clocked work in and out, and there was a 'valet' – 'a sort of general messenger for the men. He cleaned our boots, sent any message, or fetched the beer' at 10 a.m., 1 p.m. and 5 p.m.[8]

SHOPPING SPLENDOUR

The benign monotony of Poole's workshop could not have contrasted more starkly with the opulence of his showroom. During the 1880s and 90s correspondents from the trade journal *The Tailor and Cutter* returned to the shop on frequent occasions, using it as an example of best practice in retail design. The interior space of 36–39 Savile Row was strewn with artfully arranged bundles of fabric: 'one large mahogany table of magnificent build ... was heaped with black cloths, on another was placed blues, on a third greys, on another fancies, the next containing half mourning goods; while away on one side was a magnificent show case, which had been prepared and fitted up by the firm with specimens of English tailoring'. Its fitting rooms 'were miniature palaces; the pile of the carpet reminded one of rich meadow land; the decorations of the walls were one harmony of gold and satin and mirrors; the seats were cushioned in the most luxurious fashion, and the fittings of the most costly character. Moveable mirrors, adjustable electric lights, and swinging side glasses, all lent their aid ... adding to the palatial character of the apartments.'[9]

The use of extravagant displays, luxurious fittings and the latest lighting and building technology was not confined to Savile Row tailors. From the 1860s, almost all of London's major fashion traders adopted novel and eyecatching merchandising techniques. London's great international trade exhibitions in 1851 and 1862 may have contributed to this mania. The fantastical displays of fashionable commodities provided an influential template for innovative shopkeepers.[10] The proliferation of larger, more spectacular stores in the capital at this time was an extension of earlier developments in retailing custom that stretched back to the eighteenth century. It was also a reaction to the city's new incarnation as an imperial citadel, social melting-pot and financial hothouse. Shopping and spending in well-appointed surroundings were highly symbolic activities, representing London's wealth and confidence in material form, while at the same time revealing the tensions that accompanied rapid social and economic change. The journalist Albert Smith caught the resultant atmosphere in his vivid description of Regent Street (fig. 53) in 1870:

It is high noon in Regent Street. At every shop door the big-calved, gaudy-plushed footmen cluster. By every lamp post the dealers in poodles and terriers and spaniel pups congregate … Along the kerb stone itinerant vendors of prints, and stain-cleaning pastes, and mosaic gold chains and studs display their merchandise … The shops are as brilliant as they may be. How richly falls the drapery of those emblazoned shawls through the fair plate glass. How the rows of 'loves of bonnets', each upon its peg, gladdens and saddens at the same moment bright female eyes. How chastely luscious in its artistic network depend the rich clusters of precious old-fashioned lace … Everything and everybody look their best … the unchanging prints of Moyen age fashions and old scraps from Daumier's pencil in Delaporte's big window look cheerful; and the symmetrical one leg, in half a pair of buckskin breeches and a top-boot, which ornaments the shop hard by, seems positively about to hop through the window, and kick anybody who does not look happy, and flustered, and smiling and hot![11]

Regent Street remained the premier shopping street in the capital throughout this period. As London grew and its demographics shifted, other important retail districts emerged, especially in the western inner suburbs along the Brompton Road, Kensington High Street and Westbourne Grove. The City and West End saw a marked decline in their residential populations between 1851 and 1871 and, while domestic buildings were replaced with commercial ones in the centre of town, new shops were erected in locations that were more conveniently situated for those citizens who had decanted to the well-appointed brick and stucco streets beyond Hyde Park. The best known of these modern emporia was Whiteley's, 'The Universal Provider' of Bayswater, established in 1863. Haberdashery formed the base of Whiteley's business: ribbons, lace, trimmings and fancy goods. By the 1870s the store had expanded to include drapery, jewellery, imported fancy goods and such services as an estate agency, refreshment room, cleaning and dyeing department and a hairdresser. These latter additions caused much friction with established small businesses in the immediate vicinity, as well as some controversy in the press regarding the corrupting effects of fashionable consumption on young middle-class women.[12] But they also marked out Whiteley's as one of the pioneers of the department store type, that behemoth of the Victorian high street which turned shopping for clothes into a spectacular and increasingly democratic adventure. A guide book of 1887 was ecstatic with praise :

Depot, emporium, bazaar, warehouse – none of these seem to possess the slightest descriptive power. Whiteley's is an immense symposium of the arts and industries of the nation and of the world; a grand review of everything that goes to make life worth living passing in seemingly endless array before critical but bewildered humanity; an international exhibition of the resources and products of the earth and air, flood and field, established as one of the greatest 'lions' of the metropolis.[13]

New omnibus, tram and rail routes also brought consumers back into the established West End, where they could experience the more specialised provisions that London's fashion culture had to offer. By the 1880s, the most notable of these was the development of tailoring for women. The popularity of the relatively severe lines of women's 'tailor-mades' chimed with the new sense of freedom that many middle- and upper-class women were enjoying during this period. The first steps towards political suffrage saw the establishment of several women's clubs in the West End; Bedford College was founded as the first women's college of the University of London in 1878 (following the example of Newnham College, Cambridge in 1871); and the idea of the respectable career woman (as opposed to the oppressed working-class seamstress, servant and shop-girl) was gaining some ground in Fleet Street and the City, where female stenographers and secretaries began to infiltrate these traditionally male preserves. The more active lifestyles of many women, whose tastes now extended to cycling, tennis and sailing, also dictated a practical mode of dressing at odds with the decorative preciousness of much 'Paris' fashion.

Paris had become somewhat isolated during the 1870s as a result of the deprivations caused by the fall of the Second Empire and the Franco-Prussian War. It was the perfect opportunity for several London dressmakers to assert their identity as fashion leaders. The exquisite techniques of Savile Row perfectly caught the mood of the times. Redfern & Sons of Conduit Street are often

Fig. 54   Reception dress, c.1883.
Made of Liberty 'Mysore' silk by
Denyer & Co. of 28 South Street,
Worthing. The silk, hand-woven in
India. It was imported and block-
printed by Thomas Wardle of Leek
in Staffordshire and dyed 'by a per-
manent process especially for Liberty
& Co.' Most of the designs were exact
reproductions of old Indian prints.
This pattern was called 'Mooltan May
Blossom'.

credited with originating the 'man-tailored' ladies' costume, and contemporary women's magazines certainly cited his smart morning wear and outfits for fishing, hunting, shooting and driving as the coming thing. A key component of the look was the use of plain and plaid woollens
from Scotland, which further locked the trend into an enduring notion of sensible British dressing. The combination of plaids and tweeds designed for the rigours of the grouse moor and an
urbane vertical line moulded to the proportions of the city street clearly lent the clothing
designed by London-based businesses (including Redfern, H. J. Nicoll of Regent Street and
Cornhill, Joseph Smith of Bond Street and Hulbert Beech of Sloane Street) an innovative edge
equal to that achieved by other Englishmen now located in Paris such as Charles Worth and
Henry Creed. Indeed, such was Redfern's success that he soon opened branches in Paris,
Edinburgh and New York.[14]

If the tailor-mades suggested restrained practicality, the expansion of Liberty's on Regent
Street gave free rein to the more theatrical and eclectic tendencies of an emerging London

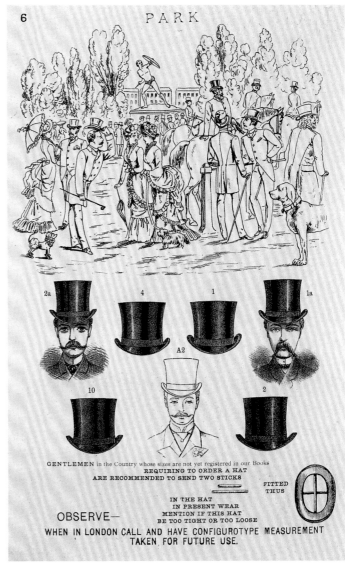

'counter-culture'. Arthur Lasenby Liberty acquired his first shop there in 1875, having built up an oriental department at Farmer & Roger's Great Shawl & Cloak Emporium nearby selling Japanese prints, lacquer, porcelain, bronzes, silks, fans and bric-à-brac inspired by the displays of eastern art at the International Exhibition of 1862. In his new venture, Liberty combined the oriental exotica he collected with the promotion of British textile goods that followed the revivalist style of pattern-making, dyeing and printing pioneered by William Morris and other arts and crafts practitioners (fig. 54). Morris was later to become a neighbour of Liberty when he set up his printing works close to the shop's at Merton Abbey near Wimbledon. By 1881, when the trend of aestheticism set in train by Liberty, Morris and their circle was lampooned in Gilbert and Sullivan's comic opera *Patience*, the store was offering 'artistic' customers the components for an entire 'aesthetic' lifestyle. A few years later, in 1884, Liberty finally opened a specialised costume department, selling items designed and made in Liberty fabrics under the directorship of influential architect and designer E. W. Godwin. Guy Bentley, one of Liberty's senior staff, recalled in his memoirs that:

> The introduction of the new department was made easier because from the earliest days of the Firm, garments from the East had formed part of the stock – such as Japanese kimonos, antique Chinese and Japanese embroidered coats and robes, Turkish veilings and shoes. During the 1880s we held annual exhibitions of embroideries, and the ladies of the

Fig. 55   'Gloucester Street – Old Clothes Market', *London: A Pilgrimage*, 1872. Blanchard Jerrold (1826–84). Engraving by A. Levasseur (exh. 1879) after Gustave Doré (1832–83).

Fig. 56   'The Park' from a catalogue for Robert Heath's hats, *c.*1882. Heath's shop was in St George's Place, near Hyde Park Corner, London. He held royal warrants from Queen Victoria, and the Prince and Princess of Wales.

Fig. 57   Court dress, 1876–8. Hand-coloured engraving after Charles Pilatte.

Department used to don Circassian, Hindoo, Japanese and Chinese attire. But the success of the new department must be attributed to the Liberty fabrics. The ladies of my youth used to speak with admiration of silk dresses which 'would stand alone'; but the designs of the Costume Department showed the beauty of soft draping lines, and this influence … has greatly modified the canons of good taste, both here and on the Continent.[15]

Liberty sold a dream of exotic and antique lands to wealthy customers. Yet the more humble clothing markets (fig. 55) of high Victorian London echoed its patterns of cultural exchange and reinvention. Whether circulating in the aristocratic West End or among the labouring classes of Bermondsey, London's fashion economy in the 1870s and 80s was marked by an excessive abundance of 'stuff' originating from all corners of the globe and fitted up to service the demands of a

THE FAST SMOKING GIRL OF THE
PERIOD.

DESCRIBED BY HERSELF.

teeming population of consumers. In his description of Rag Fair in Petticoat Lane, the American writer Daniel Kirwan captured the sublime effects achieved by clothing traders at the very bottom rung of the ladder. Their rich bounty was the result of London's unique position at the centre of a new consumerist society:

Take ... trousers that have been worn by young men of fashion, trousers without a wrinkle or just newly scoured, trousers taken from the reeking hot limbs of navvies and pot-boys, trousers from lumbering men-of-war's men, trousers that have been worn by criminals hung at Newgate, by patients in fever hospitals; waistcoats that were the pride of fast young brokers in the city, waistcoats flashy enough to have been worn ... at a racecourse ... take thousands of

Fig. 58   'The Fast Smoking Girl of the Period', *Girl of the Period Miscellany*, June 1869.

spencers, highlows, fustian jackets, some greasy some unsoiled, shooting-coats, short-coats and castaways; coats for the jockey and the dog fighter, for the peer and the pugilist, pilot jackets and sou-westers, drawers and stockings, the latter washed and hung up in all their appealing innocence, there being thousands of these garments that I have enumerated, and thousands of others that none but a master cutter could think of without a softening of the brain. Take two hundred men, women and children, mostly of the Jewish race, with here and there a burly Irishman sitting placidly smoking a pipe amid the infernal din … Take all these articles, scatter them around, hang them on nails and hooks descending from greasy stalls ascending to the old tumble down roof, and then the reader will have a dose offered to him such as I got when I fell on Rag Fair, Petticoat Lane.[16]

THE SOCIAL LABYRINTH

Victorian London's retail landscape, with its elite family firms, respectable department stores and seething street markets, made direct appeals to clearly defined segments of the population. Its wider social scene reflected a society whose demarcations according to class, occupation, wealth, race and creed were as finely detailed as they had ever been. In such a context fashion took on a heightened significance as one of the key indicators of a person's background and attitude to life, a code whose rules were ignored at the wearer's peril.

At the apex of the official social system that held sway through the whole of Queen Victoria's reign were the members of 'society'. Incorporating royalty, nobility and major and minor aristocracy, they constituted a powerful elite. During the 1830s the relative freedom of access to London's great houses and pleasure haunts was gradually tightened; a greater emphasis was placed on privacy and policing entry to clubs and public functions by a coterie of influential titled families. Exclusivity became more important. The growing potential to raise money from colonial adventuring, city deals and commercial entrepreneurship swelled the ranks of those who could afford to display their recently won riches through the traditional trophies of opulent town and country properties, accounts at the most prestigious retailers, and expensive education at the new public schools for their sons. For high society, belonging was thus further refined by wearing the 'correct' clothing and appearing in the right locations: the morning ride in Rotten Row, the private view at the Royal Academy, yachting at Cowes during early August then shooting grouse in Scotland after the 12th, hunting and country house parties in the autumn and winter months before a new round of concerts, balls and sporting events at Ascot and Henley commenced again in the spring and early summer (fig. 56).

However, the most exclusive sign of society membership was presentation at court and personal wealth was not a sufficient credential for admittance. As Leonore Davidoff explains in her important book on the workings of nineteenth-century society:

It was necessary to have a personal introduction through an individual sponsor … who had already been accepted within the royal circle … If accepted, the newcomer could then be presented to the Sovereign. These presentations took place at any special change in the … person's life. He or she was expected to visit the Sovereign on accession of office, matrimony or any kind of social or professional advancement … Drawing Rooms, where presentations were made, were attended by both men and women and it was here that women were presented both before and after marriage … By mid-century it was becoming clear that being presented to the Queen was … a 'passport to Society'.[17]

As the nineteenth century progressed, the 'coming out' of young female debutantes, experiencing their first 'season' in London and entering the marriage market, became the focal point of the whole system. Their court presentation dress, commissioned from Redfern, Worth and later on Reville & Rossiter, with its long train, white veil, and ostrich and diamond tiara epitomised the overriding sense of luxurious hauteur that pervaded the West End while the 'upper ten' were in town (fig. 57).[18]

For gentlemen as well, dressing for the circumstances of London life came with a set of rules closely tied to status and context. During the 1860s and 70s the stereotypical image of the City patriarch in black frock coat and top hat came to represent the power of capitalism, as symbolic of the age as the steam train or foggy London itself. Yet behind this seemingly constricting model, which apparently eschewed the vagaries of fashion, the respectable male consumer was presented with a framework of stylistic variations finely tuned to the differing expectations of polite society, salaried employment and personal leisure-time. The author of a popular etiquette guide of 1872 laid out the complicated options:

> Suitability equally applies to [men's] costume as to that of the ladies. For instance, when it is said that a grey suit is worn in the country, it must not be supposed that the costume is therefore suitable for every occupation and at all times of the day. You may have an invitation to a three o'clock dinner ... or to a social tea at six pm. On these occasions neither the tweed costume nor the evening dress suit would be appropriate, but the intermediate dress should be worn – a suit such as is usually donned on Sundays either in town or country – black frock coat, coloured trousers, and black tie or scarf. No attempt should ever be made to combine morning and evening dress; they should always be quite distinct, the one from the other. A black frock coat worn with black trousers is in reality as incorrect as a tail coat and coloured trousers would be.[19]

Yet as strict as the etiquette writers' guidelines on dress seemed to be, many Londoners of the period still managed to construct fashionable identities which challenged the stifling status quo, endorsing the idea that the scale and variety of the Imperial metropolis actively encouraged innovative dress. Liberty's was drawing on oriental, classical and medieval influences rather than aping high Parisian style. This novel approach found great favour with the artistic upper-middle-class residents of Kensington and Bedford Park, whose pretentious antics were mercilessly lampooned by du Maurier in *Punch* during the 1870s and 80s. It was a taste in dress and art successfully appropriated by the rising star Oscar Wilde, who probably did more than anyone to bring the 'greenery yallery' London-based cult to a wider international audience.[20] Beyond the affectations of aestheticism, the allied trend towards rational dress was personified by the German Gustave Jaeger. His shop on Regent Street purveyed a kind of anti-fashion inspired by the needs of the body. Jaeger saw London's potential as a vast market and display case to promote corset-free and sanitary clothing fit for the modern age. At the International Health Exhibition of 1884, held near the Royal Albert Hall, and in specialist London-based periodicals such as *The Rational Dress Society Gazette* and *Aglaia*, the modern concerns of comfort, hygiene and simplicity in dress were first mapped out.[21]

If aesthetic and rational dressing represented a certain radicalism in sartorial manners – sharing in a genealogy of extremist London style that includes dandyism and the subcultural dressing of the 1940s, 60s and 70s – other less avant-garde versions of mainstream fashion in the 1860s and 70s also seem to have invited controversy for their theatrical and rather shocking content. Perhaps the most notorious figure of popular London legend at this time was the 'girl of the period' (fig. 58). Inspired by the young middle-class women who flocked to new stores such as Whiteley's in Westbourne Grove or pleasure gardens like Cremorne on the Chelsea embankment, the 'girl' was a particular target of reactionary newspaper columnists. They disapproved of the freedoms which unfettered fashionable consumption appeared to bring. With her piles of false hair, brashly coloured crinolined skirts and penchant for cigarette-smoking, the young woman about town could not avoid drawing attention to herself. And consequently visitors to London such as Hippolyte Taine described an unembarrassed local engagement with fashion that stood in contradiction to the stifling tendencies of society mores, foreshadowing the provocative stance of the flapper and the dolly-bird in decades to come:

> The exaggeration of the dresses of the ladies or young girls belonging to the wealthy middle class is offensive ... Gowns of violet silk with dazzling reflections, or of starched tulle upon an expanse of petticoats stiff with embroidery ... gloves of immaculate whiteness or bright violet, golden belts with golden clasps, gold chains, hair falling back over the nape in shining masses ... the glare is terrible.[22]

SELFRIDGE'S London's New & Wonderful Shopping Centre ♫ ♫ ♫
Dedicated to Woman's Service – devoted to the Children's
Needs – the Man's Best Buying Place – with best assorted
Stocks at London's Lowest Prices:

NOW OPEN TO THE WORLD   OXFORD STREET
                                      LONDON.W.

By 1914, London's appearance had significantly altered. The hellish mid-Victorian city, dismissed by despairing critics as the 'great wen', had been transformed into an impressive modern colossus, crafted from Portland stone and stamping its authority across the British Empire. As historian Francis Sheppard comments, London was now:

> the nodal point of a colonial urban system in which the economies of the metropolis and of such distant cities as Calcutta or Sydney and their respective hinterlands complemented one another and were heavily interdependent … The status of [the] capital was very apparent in the building fabric. Gentlemen's clubs such as the East India United Service … Whitehall … stores like the Army and Navy or the Home and Colonial … South Kensington – all these were monuments to the mightiness of the Imperial metropolis.[1]

This imposing architectural landscape was serviced by efficient new technologies ranging from the telegraph and telephone to trams and underground trains. In place of the manufacturing and trading industries, which had once contributed most to London's wealth through the hard labour of East End factories, docks and warehouses, new administrative, service and communication sectors provided the wages for the majority of Londoners. London at the start of the twentieth century was, seemingly, the most confident of cities. Its bombastic faith in itself, which masked insecurities caused by such challenges to the *status quo* as the Boer War, the continuing Irish 'problem' and the spread of socialist and feminist militancy, was quite naturally reflected in the dress and demeanour of its inhabitants. Here, at least in popular memory, was a city of spruce clerks, energetic New Women, elegant actresses and dapper men-about-town whose glowing countenances, unbeknown to them, marked the passing of a golden age.

MODERN SHOPPING

In a city becoming more widely known as a centre for commerce and consumption rather than production, shopping for fashion took on a heightened importance. It was both a symbol of conspicuous leisure and a means of acquiring luxury goods which would bestow their fashionable modernity on a clientele drawn from an ever-widening social spectrum. In 1902 the journalist Mrs E. T. Cook observed both a growing addiction to the pursuit of shopping and a corresponding improvement in the retail environment as she passed through the West End:

> I am confident that if a million women of all classes could by any possibility be placed in a Palace of Truth, and interrogated straitly as to what they liked in all London, the vast majority of them would answer, 'The Shops'. Indeed, you may easily … find this out for yourself by simply taking a morning or afternoon walk down Oxford Street. Every shop of note will have its quota of would-be buyers, trembling on the brink of irrevocable purchase; its treble, nay quadruple row of admiring females, who appear to find this by far the most attractive mode of getting through the day … The shops of London have wonderfully improved in quite recent years; not perhaps so much in actual quality, as in arrangement and taste … To dress a shop-front well was in the old days hardly considered a British trait … Now even the Paris boulevard, that Paradise of good Americans, has, except perhaps in the matter of trees and wide

Fig. 59   Advertisement for the opening of Selfridge's, 1909. Drawing by Frederick Victor Poole (exh. 1891–1901).

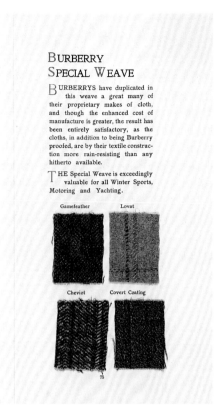

Fig. 60   'Travelling Gown', *Burberry for Ladies* (19th edn). This catalogue contains samples of the firm's fabrics, *c.*1910. American women particularly admired Burberry's country clothes and sportswear tailored in quality British fabrics.

Fig. 61   Samples of Burberry's 'special weaves', *Burberry for Ladies*, c. 1910.

Fig. 62   Advertisement for shopping at Selfridge's , 1909. Drawing by Stanley Davis. Reproduced by permission of the Selfridge's archive at HAT Archive.

streets, little to teach us. 'The wealth of Ormus and of Ind' that the shops of Regent Street and Bond Street display, their gold embroideries and wonderfully embroidered silks, tending to make a kleptomaniac out of the very elect, – these it would be hard to beat.[2]

As Mrs Cook went on to suggest, 'even the critical American cousin is now beginning to forsake Paris, and to find out the real superiority of London shops'. This increasing American interest did much to bolster the London fashion scene in the late Victorian and Edwardian eras. The rise of the 'dollar princess' – a phenomenon owing as much to the conventions of romantic fiction as to fact, whereby rich American heiresses came to England to exchange wealth for class by marrying into the needy ranks of a relatively impoverished aristocracy – certainly injected a degree of glamour and hard cash into London society, fuelling its increasingly plutocratic character. But beyond an American interest in social advancement, the influence of marketing and selling techniques honed in Chicago and New York were also making a visible impact on the practice of retailing in the capital. London writer Thomas Burke captured the changes through his description of 'a London that was going ahead. American ideas and ways of life had been infecting it for some time, and where it had been rich and fruity it was becoming slick and snappy.'[3]

Harry Gordon Selfridge, second in command at Marshall Field's department store in Chicago, was the epitome of 'slick and snappy'. When he opened his eponymous department store at the western end of Oxford Street in 1909, he was in the vanguard of Burke's Americanising trend. Selfridge's was the largest, most opulent purpose-built store the country had ever seen. Building over premises originally owned by independent drapers, milliners, tailors, hairdressers, a publican, food provisioners, tenement landlords and a school, Selfridge erected a six-acre-wide, eight-storey-high shopping palace, its façades hung with massive stone columns and the greatest expanse of plate glass in the world. The store's stock replicated the services of the traders it had obliterated, modernised according to the new theories of retail psychologists to present shopping as an unadulterated pleasure rather than routine labour. Sophisticated press advertisements announcing Selfridge's arrival in the West End trumpeted the appeal of the store's goods and facilities to the widest possible constituency. One showed 'Lady London' in billowing classical robes holding aloft a model of the new shop, proclaiming the glory of 'London's New and Wonderful Shopping Centre. Dedicated to Woman's Service – devoted to the Children's Needs – the Man's Best Buying Place – with best assorted Stocks at London's Lowest Prices: NOW OPEN TO THE WORLD' (fig. 59). In another, a fashionable young woman in picture hat and ermine muff sits with her top-hatted beau among the roses and china tea cups of Selfridge's famous restaurant, living proof of that 'shopping at Selfridge's' was 'A Pleasure – A Pastime – A Recreation' (fig. 62).[4]

Selfridge's offered the pleasures of fashionable consumption to a socially diverse audience, particularly those suburban and provincial middle- and lower middle-class women who might formerly have felt alienated by the exclusive appeal of established West End stores. The English menswear mogul Austin Reed also imported democratising American tactics in his new stores in Regent Street and Fenchurch Street. Reed had served an apprenticeship in the United States and, like Selfridge, believed in providing greater comfort to his customers. His novel advertising techniques tapped into social aspirations while ensuring that no one was put off by the elitist approach favoured by more traditional establishments. Reacting against the dark wood and funereal ambience of the typical Savile Row tailor's, Reed orchestrated a rational organisation of stock in neatly labelled boxes, carpeted rooms lined with glass display cases and informally positioned mannequins. The art nouveau glass lamps, plaster ceiling mouldings and broad polished staircases imparted an atmosphere of light, cleanliness and progressive taste which was copied by retailers across the country.

Like Selfridge, Reed was aware of advertising's enormous potential. A booklet produced by the store in 1910 called 'Types of Men & the Hat shapes that best suit them' is typical in its new psychological approach to attract custom (fig. 63). Modish line drawings ape the style of popular cartoons which appeared in men's papers of the time (by such famous draftsmen as Phil May and Charles Dana Gibson) and flatter the sensibilities of all ranks of customer. The booklet's models of hat include 'The Major' whose 'unobtrusive style make it thoroughly suitable for the man of 30 to 44'; 'The General', which 'fuller in brim and crown ... well suits a man of bigger build'; and 'Mr Justice ... a type of man in business, the professions and private life'. Drawn in bowler hats, overcoats and office suits, these urbane Londoners (perhaps the last generation to adopt hats as a matter of habit) demonstrated a confident engagement with the increasing gradations and choices now involved in city living. Their well-crafted promotional ploy recalls Thomas Burke's whimsical comment on the catalogues put out by every London store of note at the time:

> If ever I made a list of the hundred best books, number one would be an illustrated stores catalogue. What a wonderful bedside book it is! There is surely nothing so provocative to the sluggish imagination. Open it where you will, it fires an unending train of dreams. It is so full of thousands of things which you simply must have and for which you have no use at all, that you finally put it down and write a philosophic essay on the vanity of human wishes and thereby earn three guineas. Personally, I have found over a dozen short story plots in the pages of the civil service stores list.[5]

CENTURY'S END

Selfridge's and Austin Reed are key examples of the way in which some large London retailers adapted American methods in the early twentieth century. But this process of modernisation did not affect the whole of the capital's fashion industry. Alongside the democratising achievements of pioneering drapers and outfitters, the West End also supported many small bespoke businesses. Their trade relied on the traditional custom of wealthy and aristocratic patrons seeking the opulent court presentation dresses, tea gowns and tailored costumes (fig. 66) whose expense and complexity placed them firmly at the *fin de siècle*, committed to an old-world elegance all the more poignant because it could not last. Dress historian Lou Taylor has documented this lost era of couture houses, milliners and ladies outfitters and its important contribution to the blossoming of later London-based designers such as Hardy Amies and Norman Hartnell. In her study of the

Fig. 63   Illustration from Austin Reed's *Types of Men and the Hat Shapes that Best Suit Them*, 1910. Courtesy of Austin Reed.

Fig. 64 a and b   Silk evening dress, c. 1893. Made by Louise Winter of Bentinck Street, Cavendish Square, London, and decorated with net panels embroidered with gold thread and beetle wing cases from a species of jewel beetle. The panels were probably made in India. Madras was a centre for beetle-wing embroidery made for the European market.

Fig. 65 a and b   Opera coat, *c*.1895. Designed by Worth of Paris and retailed by Lewis & Allenby of Regent Street, London. Worth's designs were especially popular with American women.

Fig. 66   Woman's tailored tweed suit with a Norfolk-style jacket, *c.*1900. This suit is labelled J. R. Dale, Ladies Tailor and Habitmaker, London. In 1900 Dale's eleven shops sold men's and women's tailored garments.

Fig. 67   Embroidered wool mantle, *c.*1907. Made with panels of shirred velvet by Russell & Allen of Old Bond Street, London.

Holland Park socialites Marion Sambourne and Maud Messel, Taylor reminds us of the existence of many outlets whose products either matched or offered alternatives to the more famous Paris-designed offerings of Paquin, Worth or Redfern (all of whom had London branches) (fig. 65):

> Sarah Fullerton Monteith Young seems to have been the favourite London fashion house of Marion and her daughter Maud ... [her] bridal dress, going-away and mother-of-the-bride outfits all came from this salon in fashionable Grosvenor Square ... Maud Messel also frequented Reville & Rossiter, one of London's leading court dressmakers ... Russell & Allen, Old Bond Street, for a black lace dinner dress of about 1900–5; [and] Madame Ross, court dress maker of 19 Grafton Street and Bond Street, for [a] 1907 wool suit with ammonite buttons and for a white satin bodice with a false waistcoat front ... made from white brocade with an unusually exotic, stylised floral pattern in black, white and purple.[6]

The glamorous setting and fanciful products of London's elite dressmaking sector, dominated by women proprietors in this period, still disguised exploitative working practices. The spectre of sweating continued to haunt the trade. Philanthropists, socialists and feminist groups voiced

Fig. 68   Guide to the Daily News'
Sweated Industries Exhibition, 1906.

Fig. 69   Art class at the Shoreditch Technical Institute, 1907. (Courtesy of London Metropolitan Archives).

public concern through initiatives such as the Daily News Sweated Industries Exhibition (fig. 68), which opened at Queen's Hall Langham Place on May Day 1906 and echoed the general trend for didactic and spectacular displays, the most recent incarnation of which had been the Anglo-French exhibition held at White City the previous year. The Langham Place show aimed to educate the consumer by identifying goods made through sweated labour and exposing the conditions in which many workers were forced to live. Among the exhibits were live tableaux of men, women and children producing shirts, trousers, waistcoats, underclothes, pinafores, baby clothes, boots, shoes, trimmings, button and hook-and-eye carding, gloves, shawl fringing and bent steel for corsets. Its immediate outcome was the formation of an anti-sweating league whose activities forced Parliament to set up a commission and finally, in 1909, pass the Trade Boards Act, which established the principle of a minimum wage for the making of clothes.[7]

A further consequence of the drive to regulate the London fashion industries at the turn of the century was the development of government and industry-funded trade schools. They were designed to serve the employment needs of West End businesses and ensure that working-class girls enjoyed secure prospects at a time when destitution and prostitution were the source of serious moral panic. The schools, which eventually combined to form the present London College of Fashion in 1963, produced skilled seamstresses for court dressmaking establishments and department stores (fig. 69). The Barrett Street Trade School, situated a block away from Selfridge's, was the most prominent. It opened in 1914, offering two-year courses to fourteen- to sixteen-year-olds who studied a range of commercial processes: dressmaking, embroidery, ladies' tailoring, hairdressing, theatrical costuming, book-keeping and retailing. The classes were augmented by courses in general education, drawing and painting, and deportment and physical exercise. As an alternative to the old and inadequate system of apprenticeships or the near slave labour that existed in unregulated corners of the business, such reforms were revolutionary.[8]

THEATRICAL DISPLAY

While Barrett Street girls engaged in amateur theatricals and trained in the manufacture of wigs and costumes for the stage, the professional actresses who benefited from their enhanced creative skills emerged during the 1890s and 1900s as icons of a new London style of dressing. More than any other social type, the late Victorian and Edwardian actress epitomised the overblown, highly theatrical sartorial rhetoric of the moment. The Italian journalist Mario Borsa noted the ubiquitous presence of theatrical personalities in the city. In 1908 he wrote that 'the cult of the actor and the actress is a new development – of the nature of Carlyle's "hero worship". The actor looms large in the public eye. London lies at his feet. His portrait is everywhere – at the photographer's, the bookseller's, on posters, picture postcards, and even on table services and other articles of china.'9 But it was as prototypical fashion icon that the London actor and actress really excelled.

The theatre was able to exert a considerable influence on fashionable taste in two principal ways from the 1880s. A shift in the nature of West End entertainment made the medium more accessible to a broad audience where formerly its attractions had been largely restricted to niche customers. Theatrical entrepreneurs such as John Hollingshead, George Edwardes, Richard

Fig. 70   Cape said to have been worn by Lily Langtry, 1890s. Made of wool cloth decorated with appliqués of corded silk and glass beads.

Figs. 71 a and b   Programmes for London's Gaiety Theatre, 1903.

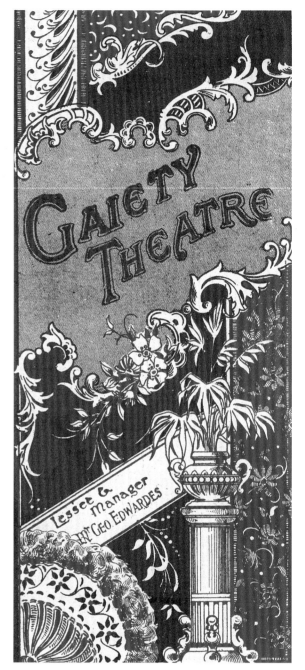

D'Oyly Carte and Sir Charles Wyndham recognised the financial sense in sponsoring productions whose spectacular sets, glamorous contemporary costumes and uncontroversial but timely themes would draw the biggest crowds, including, importantly, single women, for whom the stigma of attending the theatre had been removed. Where formerly risqué burlesques, ponderous classics and extraordinarily lavish pantomimes had split audiences along the lines of men about town, high-brow seekers after culture and families with children, the new medium of modern melodrama and musical comedy had something to offer all. When presented in the comfortable and elegant surroundings of newly built theatres such as the Coliseum and supported by all the paraphernalia of the expanding promotional industries (with sophisticated posters and programmes and a renewed transport and catering infrastructure all making trips to the West End more of an event), the up-to-date 'show' could not fail to be a creative and marketing success.

Musical comedy was perhaps the most explicitly 'fashionable' of the new theatrical forms.

Associated closely with the famous Gaiety Theatre on the Strand, many of the shows in this genre chose contemporary settings such as the department store, the entertainment industry or the fashion house in which to set light romantic narratives that depended for their appeal on catchy songs, an attractive chorus line and well-known leading actors (fig. 71). The most dramatic departure made by the producers of musical comedy was in the realm of costume. As one theatrical memoirist put it: 'Tights were banned and Bruton Street frocks and Savile Row coats . . . were substituted for the costumes which the wardrobe mistresses or Covent Garden costumiers had run up for earlier Vaudeville players.'[10] A typical example of the trend was the production *In Town*, staged by George Edwardes at the Gaiety in 1892. As a reviewer noted:

> Some very, very smart frocks are worn by the 'chorus ladies of the Ambiguity Theatre' in the first act, Miss Maud Hobson being well to the fore in the way of style and presence. Her dress . . . is quite the smartest I have seen for some time. The skirt, which is made in a demi-train, lined underneath (and seen only when the wearer moved) with pale pink silk, was composed of a beautiful shade of dove coloured silk – over this was worn a bodice of the richest purple velvet, designed in a new and very quaint manner, the fronts being cut very long so as to form kind of tabs . . . Miss Hobson wears with this dress a large spoon-shaped bonnet with a black velvet bow . . . The eyes of many of the female portion of the audience grew large with envy as they watched this creation and its tall and graceful wearer move about the stage.[11]

As the review suggests, members of the audience were encouraged to approach the spectacle of contemporary fashion arranged on stage as a model for what might be achievable in everyday life. Historian Peter Bailey characterises musical comedy as a regulatory social device, controlling the unruly desires of a largely female and lower-middle-class audience, whilst encouraging then towards an unthinking consumption of fashionable products. Yet, he also notes:

> within a generation . . . London women came to use the greater range of cheap consumer goods in ways that not only followed the promptings of popular fashion and femininity but realised a more independent sense of self. Although a blithely manipulative mode, musical comedy may have stimulated such new imaginative gains for women in a more overtly sexualised identity that was no longer merely hostage to the designs of men.[12]

This circumventing of patriarchal control and celebration of a feminised consumerist desire was also a strategy promoted through the second fashion-related innovation associated with London theatre at the *fin de siècle*. This was the rise of the celebrity player, whose own tastes and character were often more acclaimed than their stage roles. Actors and actresses from all walks of theatrical life enjoyed a new prominence as fashion plates and postcard pin-ups around the turn of the century. London stars including Lily Langtry (fig. 70), George Alexander, Marie Tempest, Constance Collier, Marie Lloyd, Vesta Tilley and Maurice Chevalier were all noted for their individual take on fashion, and celebrities such as Mary Moore often capitalised on the marketing potential offered by a link with Paris and London's elite garment trades.

Moore featured in the genteel 'drawing room' plays put on at Wyndham's Theatre, which she managed with her husband Sir Charles Wyndham. She paid close attention to dressing in all the productions with which she was involved, developing sound business partnerships with various couture houses who shared her belief that the stage provided 'the finest medium for dressmakers to advertise their wares'.[13] Beer, Doeuillet and Lacroix and other Parisian designers contributed to plays including *The Liars* (1898) and *The Mollusc* (1908), and in the case of the latter production Moore even went to the lengths of re-upholstering the interior of the Criterion Theatre to match the Nattier-blue chiffon-velvet of her gown. French companies would also discount items that Moore promised to wear at prestigious social events such as Ascot. The actress recalled that 'for these occasions I generally had two or three dresses sent over from Worth's Paris House, which as they had my pattern over there – arrived ready to put on, without all the trouble of fitting. How delightful it was to receive such lovely gowns at a special *prix d'artiste*. In those days one could afford to dress well!'[14]

Mary Moore generally deferred to Paris as the home of sartorial innovation, but she also

Fig. 72   Gertie Millar in *The Quaker Girl*, 1910. She is wearing a dress designed by Lucile.

turned to that most infamous of London dressmakers, Lucile (Lady Duff Gordon) for the costume designs of *The Physician* in 1897. She recounted a particular coat 'of black charmeuse, covered with sequins and lined with ermine which showed when she moved', adding that 'I used to go and look at it growing under Madame Lucile's direction, and my only criticism each time was "more sequins", as I wanted the material completely covered, as I had seen it on the French stage'.[15] Lucile also designed for Gertie Millar, the Bradford-born star who became George Edwardes' leading lady at the Gaiety in 1901. *The Quaker Girl* of 1910, one of her most successful plays, ran for 536 performances (fig. 72), and Lucile later donated a model based on one of the dresses Gertie Millar wore in the play to the Museum of London.[16]

Lucile was adept at producing diaphanous, shimmering gowns which fell provocatively somewhere between lingerie and evening dress (fig. 73). In her elegant grey salon at 17 Hanover Square, her characterful clothes were modelled on statuesque mannequins who answered to the names of Gamela, Dolores, Phyllis and Hebe as they performed in innovative tableaux titled 'the sighing sound of lips unsatisfied' or 'red mouth of a venomous flower'. In this manner Lucile

Fig. 73   Design for an evening dress by Lucile, c.1910. Hand-coloured lithograph. Samples of the fabrics from which it was made have been stuck to the mount.

Fig. 74   *Piccadilly at Night, c.1893.*
Oil painting by Edward Dudley Heath
(*c.*1886–1940).

effectively blurred the boundaries between fashion and theatre. From 1910 she expanded her
business to New York, where she went on to dress the Ziegfield Follies, Paris and Chicago, and set
a powerful precedent for later traditions of showing couture in Europe and America. She also
captured the sense of theatricality, scandal and sensualism that inflected the fashion culture of
London between the last years of Queen Victoria and the onset of the First World War. In her own
modest words, Lucile 'had a message for the women I dressed. I was the first dressmaker to bring
joy and romance into clothes, I was a pioneer. I loosed upon a startled London, a London of flannel underclothes ... a cascade of chiffons, of draperies as lovely as those of ancient Greece.'[17]

ON THE STREETS

The London of flannel underclothes was perhaps more grounded in reality than Lucile's dream of
Grecian nymphs. It was in the dressing habits of everyday Londoners of the period that some of
the most enduring stereotypes of the London spirit found their origins. As the City of London
developed to become the engine of imperialist expansion in the last quarter of the nineteenth

century, the changing figure of the office worker (see Chapter Two) came to dominate the urban landscape. His seemingly conservative attire is easy to overlook in the street photographs and *cartes de visite* of the time, but in many ways the ready-made lounge suit and stiff collar and tie that constituted the clerk's occupational uniform is as symbolic of London's modernity as the daring sparkle of Mayfair dressing. In a book of 1908 fittingly titled *City of the World*, the London writer Edwin Pugh produced a devastating caricature of the type:

> His feet are big and clumsy: cheap ill-fitting boots account for that ... One suspects from a certain slackness and abrupt bulginess about his sleeves and the legs of his trousers that his joints are disproportionately large ... If his hair is ... dark, then he plasters it down tightly on his scalp to a brilliant sleekness and finishes off his coiffure with a slimy arc upon his forehead ... He is not well dressed, but he is at least decently clad in ready made clothes, or clothes made to measure by some cheap cash tailor. Indeed he reeks of cheapness ... He has suitable clothes for every occasion, even evening clothes sometimes – but they are all of a like shoddy quality, and seem all to have been made for somebody else. And the effect of his big hands and big feet, his stringy sinewy neck and loosely hung limbs, is to accentuate this distressing element of cheapness and tawdriness.[18]

Fig. 75   The Suffragette look: postcard showing members of the Women's Social and Political Union, *c*.1908. *Front row*: Mary Gawthorpe (in a dark dress), Christabel Pankhurst, Mrs Pethick-Lawrence, Annie Kenney (middle to right). *Back row*: Dorothy Pethick (far left), Jessie Kenney (far right).

Fig. 76   Holywell Street, Strand,
looking west, 1900. Detail of a watercolour by Philip Norman (1842–1931).

Pugh's snobbish distaste for the appearance and values of the clerk was not unusual. The growing ranks of the lower middle-classes who occupied the new suburbs of neat terraced houses now
circling the centre of London seemed, in the artistic and bohemian imagination of the period, to
threaten the sense of freedom and innovation that intellectuals valued in city life. The Grossmith
brothers' famous satire of petit-bourgeois life in 1890s Holloway, serialised in *Punch* as *The Diary
of a Nobody* took a similarly condescending view of the new administrative class. But behind the
sneering, what such texts reveal are the powerful anxieties which the clerk figure was able to
inspire. His gangly body and sedentary occupation stoked eugenicist fears about a decline in the
physical strength of the nation and a possible collapse of empire, a fear played out in public
debates about the British army's lack of fitness to fight in the Boer War. His access to a wide
range of cheap and tawdry mass-produced clothes suggested the corrupting influence of a
democratised fashion culture. Nowhere was the allure of this culture more in evidence than in
the realm of music hall. Here, in the smoky halls of Leicester Square, home to the famous Empire,
and south and east London, working-class men and women and 'slumming' clerks and aristocrats
found a lively setting for acts of sartorial outrage, both on and off the stage. An account of 1890
captures the attractions of the genre:

The Eastender has created his idea [of glamour] from a gentleman or 'gent' of which he has had glimpses at the bars and finds it in perfection at his music hall. At the music hall, everything is tinselled over; and we find a kind of racy gin-born affectation to be the mode, everyone being 'dear boy' or a 'pal' . . . There is a suggestion of perpetual dress suit, with deep side pockets, in which the hands are ever plunged; indeed a true gentleman will rather hire his suit for the occasion – always costly and involving a deposit – rather than fail in these conveniences. And we must ever recollect to strut and stride rather than walk.[19]

Regardless of his critics, the clerk clearly embodied much that was forward-looking about London at the turn of the century. His figure in its modern clothing strode resolutely forward into the twentieth century. Partnering him in this endeavour was the character of the 'new woman', a stereotype whose associated imagery was also closely linked to the worlds of fashion and clothing. In some ways it is more difficult to establish a direct association between the new woman and the specific environment of London. The modern ideal of progressive femininity, captured most evocatively by the American cartoonist Charles Gibson in her neat blouse, swirling skirt and straw boater, emerged simultaneously in New York, Paris, Barcelona, London, Berlin and other western capitals during the 1890s. Like the clerk, her form was bracketed with modern pursuits such as cycling and new careers such as stenography and teaching, and her costume followed suit with an emphasis on practicality: items were generally easier to clean and maintain, and with less reliance on corsetry and skirt supports, the potential for free movement was considerably enhanced.

Occasionally, however, the New Woman did seem to embody the particular spirit of London. The activities of suffrage movements such as the Women's Social and Political Union (WSPU), the Artists' Franchise League and the Women's Freedom League saw to it that the struggle for emancipation was rooted both in a discourse of metropolitan fashionability and within the physical borders of the West End. Historians such as Lisa Tickner and Erika Rappaport have noted that 'when the WSPU chose colours as the symbols for their movement, they essentially branded their cause and sought to capture that "appeal to the eye" that Edwardian window dressers, set designers, and advertisers believed was so essential to successful selling' (fig. 75).[20] Beyond the adoption of purple, white and green rosettes, hat bands and posies by campaigners, such symbolism extended to a complex engagement between suffragettes and London's fashion retailers. It veered from the placing of advertisements by Whiteley's and others in the suffrage journal *Votes for Women*, to the infamous window-smashing campaign of March 1912 in which activists targeted major West End department stores. This active incorporation of fashion into the political and social life of a greater number of Londoners than ever before was the legacy left by an Edwardian milieu that has otherwise been characterised as complacent, nostalgic and backward-looking. After the First World War, the stirrings of rebellion initiated by suffragettes, actresses and clerks resulted in the spectacular flowering of subcultural and counter-cultural movements that have marked the development of London fashion in the twentieth century.

When the matinee idol Rudolph Valentino paid a flying visit to London in 1923, he and his wife Natacha Rambova set aside time for sightseeing and shopping. As well as visiting the Tower of London, Westminster Abbey, Windsor Castle and Hampton Court, there was 'much rushing to tailors, bootmakers, hatters, shirtmakers, etc.' for, as Rambova remarked, 'London is to men what Paris is to women – the paradise of fashion shops'.[1] In terms of consumption, this dichotomy was undoubtedly true, but commentators at the time felt that fashion itself had changed. Sartorial borrowings between England and France had been taking place for centuries, but after the First World War, with international high society travelling *en masse* according to the season, the adoption of common tastes at an elite level was inevitable.[2]

The make-up of high society was also changing. High rank was no longer a prerequisite for membership. Talent, intelligence, wealth or merely being 'good value' might equally provide an entrée. As the writer Barbara Cartland remarked, society in the 1920s was a 'pot pourri of the titled, the beautiful, the famous and notorious, all welded together with money'.[3] Though small, this group attracted intense media coverage, diffusing its trendsetters' fashions across a wide public.

LONDON AND PARIS

Paris remained the dominant influence on womenswear design in Britain during and after the First World War. However, English tastes informed much of the clothing made in London. These were dictated by the lifestyle of the upper classes who moved from town to country according to the social calendar. Considerations of suitability and practicality guided their choice of fabric and cut as much as fashion. Too keen an interest in fashion was still equated by some with superficiality, and even British *Vogue*, under the editorship of the intellectual Dorothy Todd, reflected these lingering beliefs. In 1922 it recommended: 'The happy medium, the adaptation of costume to character and condition (always with an eye to the prevailing trend or trends of the times), is safe, smart sanity, and wise vanity to boot.'[4]

But is there any evidence of a metropolitan style or taste? London remained a centre for alternative, 'artistic' dressing, and consumer choice burgeoned with the revival of interest in handcrafted textiles and the establishment of specialist shops. The period also saw the emergence of the first of a number of young designers who wanted international recognition and who, like Lucile, made London their base. The most successful were Norman Hartnell and the now largely forgotten Isobel. Both were determined to be accepted as British designers, but neither was inward-looking and their designs reflected English sensibilities through an urban lens. However they initially lost orders because of their nationality. As Hartnell famously remarked, 'I suffered from the unforgivable disadvantage of being English in England.'[5]

Why did London-based dressmakers find it so difficult to establish themselves as original designers on a par with Parisian couturiers? The overwhelming bias of the British press from *Vogue* to *Mabs Fashions* (fig. 89), a cheap monthly magazine read by middle-class housewives and working girls, was towards Paris (fig. 79). French fashions were described in detail and individual houses credited with the endless stream of novelties the public had come to expect from across the Channel. When *Vogue* did cover the London fashions in the late teens and early twenties, the

Fig. 77   Detail of fig. 87, silk chiffon evening dress decorated with sequins and seed beads, retailed by Marshall & Snelgrove, *c*.1925.

sources of the clothes were often anonymous. Not surprisingly, copies of Paris models, however distant from the original, inspired greater confidence than their London-designed counterparts. There was also a perception that the culture and physical environment of London, and of Britain generally, was not conducive to artistic inspiration. Isobel contrasted the 'sparkling atmosphere' of Paris to the depressing 'spectacle of thousands of blue-nosed mackintosh clad women fighting their way through Wagnerian floods and tempests' in London. But her analysis of the problems English designers faced went deeper than the weather. In France, fashion was taken seriously both as an art and an industry. With the encouragement of the Chambre Syndicale de la Couture Parisienne, designers and textile manufacturers co-operated, providing each other with mutual inspiration and the raw materials for a well-designed product. Isobel's pertinent recommendation that a society be formed to promote the interests of British couturiers would not be realised until the outbreak of the Second World War.[6]

CHALLENGING PARIS: ISOBEL AND HARTNELL

Both Isobel and Norman Hartnell were self-taught designers who started their careers as fashion artists, in Isobel's case as a schoolgirl. She claimed that her earnings provided the capital to set herself up as a dressmaker in a top floor room in Regent Street when she left school. Within about four years, she had moved in 1919 to a corner site on the junction of Regent Street and Maddox Street, and by 1921 was taking full-page advertisements in British *Vogue* and had a

Fig. 78   *The Visits of Veronica*, 1929. A Marshall & Snelgrove catalogue advertising dress and accessories.

Fig. 79   Advertisement for Paquin's London branch at 39 Dover Street, 1921. The house was located in Paris in the Rue de la Paix. (Bassano Advertising Archive, Museum of London).

A THREE-PIECE SPORTS SUIT BY ISOBEL. PRICE 12 GNS.

Isobel

223 REGENT STREET, W.1
& at HARROGATE
(ONLY ADDRESSES)

branch in the fashionable North Yorkshire town of Harrogate. She described herself as a court dressmaker and sold presentation dresses, gowns, tailored garments and millinery. She was best known for furs and sportswear, which she exported to America and designed with her American clients in mind. Her collection for autumn/winter 1928 included a 'dull sea-water green' jersey dress with a scarf collar of striped crêpe de chine and matching opossum-trimmed coat (designed for motoring to lunch in the country) and a three-piece brown and red flecked tweed costume worn with a diagonally cut jumper for autumn race meetings. The clothes were well-tailored, supremely wearable, totally appropriate and chic – a quality associated with the *mondaine*: English women with English tastes aspired instead to look pretty or becoming.[7] 'No one but Madame Isobel could give the particular interpretation to the mode which she succeeds in doing' (fig. 80).[8] By 1933 Isobel employed a staff which, with four hundred girls, fifty men and fifteen mannequins, far outnumbered most London court dressmakers. Some employed over a hundred but the average was ten to thirty workers.[9] No garments designed by Isobel are known to survive in the larger British museum collections.

Isobel's London salon was decorated in grey and featured a black marble staircase which added a glamorous theatricality to her mannequin shows. A staircase also featured in a short film about Isobel made for *Eve's Film Review* in 1932.[10] Pathé Frères launched *Eve's Film Review* in 1921 as part of the supporting programme at their cinemas. The subject matter reflected women's magazines of the period and fashion, usually French, was a leading topic. Pathé anticipated that

Fig. 80   Advertisement for a three-piece sports suit by Isobel, August 1928.

Fig. 81   McCall's paper pattern for coats, 1928. McCall was an American pattern company.

their 'kinema going Eves' would be influenced by the clothes they saw; the films were directed to show garments from different angles with close-ups of details and accessories. [11] The films were also aspirational. As Isobel's model sauntered languidly down the staircase to reveal the 'exquisite' flesh pink georgette evening gown worn under her fur-trimmed pink and gold moiré coat, the cinemagoer might have fantasised that she was at the show, ticking the outfit as a potential purchase. The black and white film is silent, but the intertitles imitate the manner of the *vendeuse* who introduced the models. The film may have been triggered by the coverage Isobel received when she designed a free pattern for a street frock (ideally made in British woven Viyella) for readers of the *Sunday Pictorial*, in support of the government's 'Buy British' campaign in 1932. [12] Dress patterns, whether produced by pattern companies or issued under the auspices of women's magazines, were, like film, another way in which fashion was disseminated across income bands, class and national borders (fig. 81).

The 1920s was a decade dominated by youth. Although the young and rich rejected the formal, planned, social life of their elders in favour of a restless round of nightclubs, impromptu parties and casual invitations, the conventional rights of passage, such as presentation at court and the society wedding, remained unchallenged. For these occasions, Norman Hartnell was the designer of choice. His romantic, feminine presentation gowns and dance dresses, typically made of silk or tulle sprinkled with beads and sequins (fig. 82), were the perfect antidote to the neat, androgynous, democratic *garçonne* look that typified the daywear of the period. The picturesque qualities of Hartnell's designs appealed to English sensibilities, but he was also in touch with the times and his preference for working with soft fabrics accorded perfectly with the contemporary ideal of looking young and casual. As *Vogue* remarked: 'This clever young designer has a new and youthful attack. His clothes express the vagaries as well as the careless chic of a wayward smart generation.' [13] Barbara Cartland, who wrote a gossip column for the *Daily Express* in the mid-1920s, was an early supporter. She introduced friends to him in return for clothes at cost price and wore Hartnell designs for her court presentation in 1926 and her wedding. Other debutantes dressed by him included the photographer Cecil Beaton's sister, Nancy in 1928, and in 1930, Lady Bridgett Poulett, Rose Bingham and Margaret Whigham. His reputation for dressing 'some of the loveliest women in London' guaranteed him extensive media coverage and enhanced his reputation as London's rising star. [14]

Hartnell's facility for drawing had encouraged him to study architecture at Cambridge University, but his studies suffered from his involvement with the university's amateur dramatic societies. During his second year, in 1922, Minnie Hogg, a journalist who wrote for the London *Evening Standard* under the pseudonym Corisande, noticed the costumes he had designed for a Footlights review. With her support, Hartnell dropped out to try his luck as a designer and sketch artist but, after having his work pirated by Lucile, he determined to set up on his own. With financial help from his family and the damages he won from suing Lucile he opened his own salon a year later, occupying the two top floors at 10 Bruton Street in Mayfair. As he later remarked, 'No house was ever started in a more unprofessional, amateurish way', but in spite of his inexperience, his first show in March 1924 was a critical success. [15] Securing clients was more problematic as most English women preferred to wear French designer labels. Undeterred, he decided the way to establish his name was to show in Paris as a London-based British designer. His first venture in 1927 was not a commercial success, but it attracted the attention of Main Bocher, the editor-in-chief of French *Vogue*, who praised the beauty of the collection while deploring the workmanship. His breakthrough came the following year when Canadian and US customers bought from his collections and from then on his advertisements situate him in both cities.

The stars of the Edwardian stage had a huge influence on young men growing up before the war. For both Norman Hartnell and Cecil Beaton, the vaudeville artist Gaby Delys was the epitome of glamour. Her jewels were legendary and she offset her abundant personal charms with lavish furs and exotic feathers. Beaton once watched her drive by in her Rolls-Royce which left 'a scented trail of unbelievable luxury and allure, spiced with a breath of naughtiness that escaped, at least by a narrow margin, being trashy'. [16] As a young man, Hartnell sketched her and was entranced by her many costume changes in *Suzette*. His love of the stage never left him, and his

Fig. 82   Silk satin evening dress, c.1925. Designed by Norman Hartnell and embroidered in 'Chinese architectural style' with sequins, artificial pearls and gold thread. The dress is labelled 'Norman Hartnell 10 Bruton St. W.'

designs incorporated many of the fabrics and trimmings associated with the theatre. Naturally he siezed the opportunity to design for the stage. Working with actresses gave him and other designers the chance to dress more sophisticated sexy women and the prospect of abundant free publicity. One of his earliest theatrical successes starred Lily Elsie, an Edwardian actress dressed by Lucile before the war. *The Theatre World* found the play's love interest, provided by Elsie and Ivor Novello, insipid, but praised *The Truth Game's* well-observed comic interludes which allowed the leading lady time to change into yet another outfit.[17] *Vogue*, in an article subtitled 'The Smartest Stage Clothes Have the Greatest Off-Stage Chic', ignored the plot and stressed the synergy between designer and star. 'Aided and abetted by [Hartnell], Miss Elsie achieves what one may call smartness to the "nth" degree; the smartness of luxury.'[18]

SOCIETY SHOPKEEPERS

The First World War triggered sweeping changes in British society. Three quarters of a million of the country's young men died and of those who returned many were disabled, creating a huge surplus of unmarried women. The country was in debt and the economy unstable. Unemployment rose to two million by the end of 1921, and the aristocracy had to sell land and property to make ends meet. The 1919 Sex Disqualification Act opened up some professions, including the Bar, for educated women, but the less well-qualified had to look elsewhere. Many upper-class women resorted to shopkeeping, selling everything from dogs and antiques to hats and clothing.[19] The most notorious was Christabel Russell, daughter-in-law of the second Baron Ampthill, whose wife was a Lady of the Bedchamber to Queen Mary. Accused by her husband of conceiving a child in adultery, she fought a three-year legal battle to clear her name and establish her son's legitimacy.

Christabel had had a liberal, unconventional upbringing, but she was also a product of the war which accustomed her to independence. By day she had worked at the Woolwich Arsenal, and then for the Whitworth Engineering Company, where she earned £400 a year as managing secretary; at night she indulged her passion for dancing with a string of admiring partners. The Ampthills were not wealthy and in 1920, to the horror of her in-laws, Christabel and her mother, a skilled needlewoman, set up a dress shop in Curzon Street, where she and her estranged husband also lived.[20] Christabel's business flourished on an irresistible combination of notoriety, talent and hard work. She advertised clothing for the London season, and as a keen horsewoman, specialised in riding habits. As well as creating her own designs for clients who wanted something individual, she, like many other dressmakers at the elite level, sold Paris models by Poiret, Lanvin and Louise Boulanger.

Lady Victor Paget, daughter-in-law of the sixth Marquess of Anglesey, was another successful society dressmaker. In 1925, she opened a shop in Grafton Street next door to Chez Victor, a popular nightclub named after its proprietor Victor Perosino. As a member of the London social scene, she was regularly photographed for *Vogue* modelling clothes from her own collections and giving her house double exposure. Sketched by Cecil Beaton, her angular features and smart casual style recall Coco Chanel's appearance. She sold Chanel models alongside her own designs and the packaging and name of her first perfume, 'Lady Victor Paget No. 1', suggest that she encouraged the comparison. She also designed for actresses. A pyjama suit made for Hilda Moore, who played a blackmailer in the 1927 play *Interference*, survives at the Museum of London (fig. 83).[21] Reporting on the 1929 London collections, *Vogue* raved: 'Lady Victor, a crisply brittle brunette, has exquisite taste, and her collection is a revelation. Most of her garments should be sent to the London Museum as typical specimens of the best clothes of to-day, so that future generations could discover with amazement to what an art of restrained and subtle elaboration dressmaking had soared in 1929.'[22]

RUSSIAN SHOPS, AMERICAN STORES

During the first two decades of the twentieth century, Russia exerted a strong influence on fashion and interior decoration in the West. The exotic plots, sets and costumes of the Ballets Russes unleashed a vogue for quasi-oriental styles, but the late nineteenth-century Slav revival, which

Fig. 83 a and b   Pyjama suit designed by Lady Victor Paget and worn by Hilda Moore in the 1927 play *Interference*. The jacket is made from printed silk velvet, the trousers from silk satin.

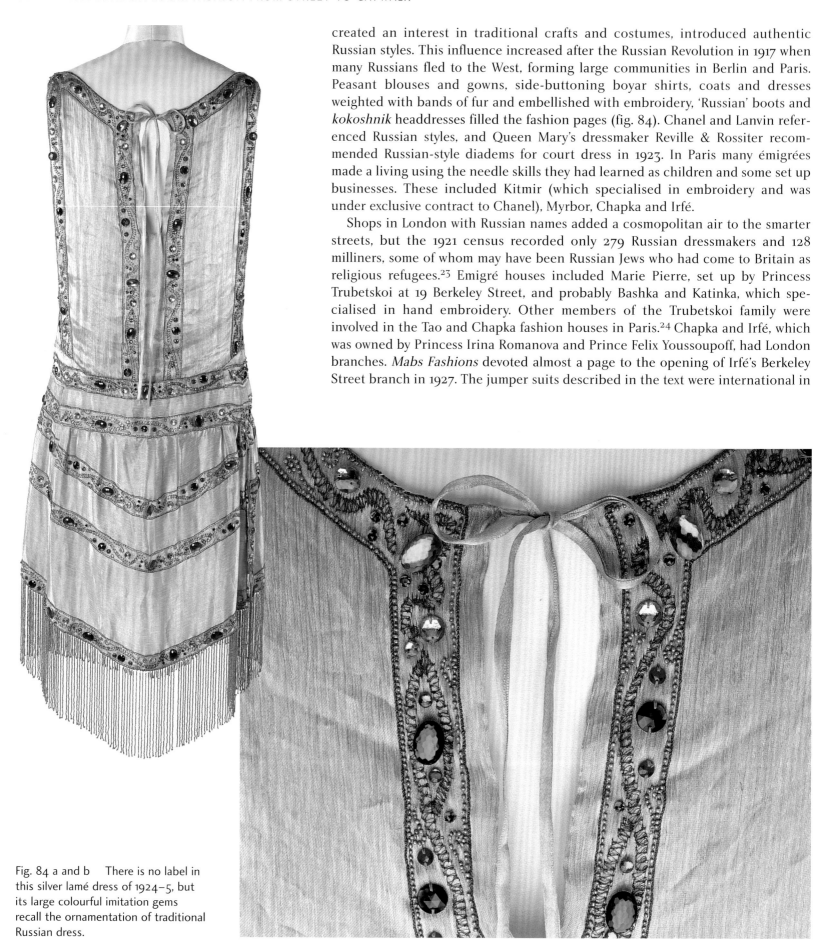

created an interest in traditional crafts and costumes, introduced authentic Russian styles. This influence increased after the Russian Revolution in 1917 when many Russians fled to the West, forming large communities in Berlin and Paris. Peasant blouses and gowns, side-buttoning boyar shirts, coats and dresses weighted with bands of fur and embellished with embroidery, 'Russian' boots and *kokoshnik* headdresses filled the fashion pages (fig. 84). Chanel and Lanvin referenced Russian styles, and Queen Mary's dressmaker Reville & Rossiter recommended Russian-style diadems for court dress in 1923. In Paris many émigrées made a living using the needle skills they had learned as children and some set up businesses. These included Kitmir (which specialised in embroidery and was under exclusive contract to Chanel), Myrbor, Chapka and Irfé.

Shops in London with Russian names added a cosmopolitan air to the smarter streets, but the 1921 census recorded only 279 Russian dressmakers and 128 milliners, some of whom may have been Russian Jews who had come to Britain as religious refugees.[23] Emigré houses included Marie Pierre, set up by Princess Trubetskoi at 19 Berkeley Street, and probably Bashka and Katinka, which specialised in hand embroidery. Other members of the Trubetskoi family were involved in the Tao and Chapka fashion houses in Paris.[24] Chapka and Irfé, which was owned by Princess Irina Romanova and Prince Felix Youssoupoff, had London branches. *Mabs Fashions* devoted almost a page to the opening of Irfé's Berkeley Street branch in 1927. The jumper suits described in the text were international in

Fig. 84 a and b   There is no label in this silver lamé dress of 1924–5, but its large colourful imitation gems recall the ornamentation of traditional Russian dress.

style, but the gossipy description of the Youssoupoffs, with their seductive mix of high rank, tragedy and Eastern luxury, has a cinematic quality:

> Princess Youssoupoff, who is a niece of the late Tsar of Russia, was there, gowned in black with a touch or two of gold. She chatted to some of her personal friends and new clients in a cleverly contrived balcony room which had adorable little windows, curtained with pale yellow taffeta, overlooking the showroom beneath, where Prince Youssoupoff, dark, distinguished, and rather sad-looking 'received'.[25]

The huge department stores in Oxford Street and Regent Street formed a stark contrast to the discreet dressmaking and tailoring establishments to the south and west. Battling for customers, the stores continued to expand physically and corporately, with Debenham's buying Marshall & Snelgrove in 1919, and Harrod's acquiring Dickins & Jones (fig. 85) and Swan & Edgar. The latter was completely rebuilt using the latest technology during the redevelopment of Regent Street and reopened in 1927 with fifty departments and a clean modern frontage on Piccadilly Circus. Three years earlier, Selfridge's had opened its western extension, giving it three and a half acres of floor space in the basement alone, and Peter Robinson in Oxford Street also expanded. The 1920s were the heyday of these department stores: within a few years, the costs of maintaining the massive buildings and such high levels of customer service and marketing in an overcrowded market were no longer sustainable.

The design and scale of these stores in their prime were based on the American model, and Oxford Street effectually became London's 'Main Street'. In 1933 it was served by thirty-nine bus

Fig. 85   Black satin shoes purchased from Dickins & Jones, c.1925. Decorated with cut-steel beads and sequins.

Fig. 87 a and b (*above*)   Silk chiffon evening dress retailed by Marshall & Snelgrove, *c*.1925. Decorated with sequins and seed beads. The mock drapery over the hips and stylised fan-shaped flowerheads reflect the fad for Egyptian styles prompted by the discovery of Tutankhamen's tomb in November 1922.

Fig. 86 (*facing*)   'Oxford Street', *Rues et visages de Londres*, 1928. Pierre Mac Orlan (1882–1970). Hand-coloured etching by Charles Laborde (1880–1941).

routes and four underground railway lines connected to an expanding overground network of buses, trams and trains bringing shoppers in from the populous suburbs (fig. 86).[26] The north side of the street was lined with huge stores with imposing façades and lavishly appointed interiors. Yet in spite of their glamorous fashion shows and genteel facilities, in reality most catered for the middle market or, in the case of Selfridge's and Bourne & Hollingsworth, the 'general trade'. The overall emphasis was on choice and value, with smartness and practicality valued above fashion. Writers homed in on crowds of the window-shoppers, mocking their rapt scrutiny of the plaster mannequins who beckoned to them like sirens and whose appearance contrasted so vividly with their own innate dowdiness:

Reality and idealism walk hand in hand along the smooth pavements of Oxford Street. Reality and idealism also face each other through the thin sheets of plate-glass . . . In vain does the

Fig. 88   The ladies' tailoring workroom at Barrett Street, photographed
for the 1927–8 school prospectus. The
students are learning to make made-
to-measure tailored clothing. (Courtesy
of London College of Fashion,
University of the Arts London).

customer have the article fetched from the window; it is never the same. It can never be the same. The illusion of the shop-window belongs to a kind of fairy magic, and that territory behind the glass is a fairyland into which mere mortals cannot penetrate.[27]

Top department stores – Marshall & Snelgrove, Harrod's, Harvey Nichols – maintained work-rooms where custom-made French models were produced alongside their own designs (fig. 87). They recruited staff from the recently established needle-trade schools organised on the lines of the French *écoles professionelles* to train girls to work in the couture trade making handcrafted clothing. By the 1920s, many of the students at the Barrett Street Trade School (see Chapter Four) were Jewish, and many had lost fathers in the war (fig. 88).[28] The school committees included representatives from court dressmakers, such as Mrs Handley-Seymour and Reville & Rossiter, and from Liberty's, Jay's, Harvey Nichols, Selfridge's and Marshall & Snelgrove. The ready-made clothing sold by department stores might be produced on the premises or off-site. Some stores, like Hitchcock Williams & Company in St Paul's Churchyard, had their own factories; others worked with East End manufacturers or wholesalers. Taken together, the bespoke and wholesale dressmaking trade employed about 57,000 workers, of whom 95% were women or girls. The wholesale branch ranged from large factories of three and four hundred workers to small, often Jewish-run workshops with three or four staff.[29] Tailoring was classified as a separate branch of the industry and ladies' tailoring accounted for about a third of the trade.

DEMOCRATISATION OF CLOTHING

The fashions of the twenties were ideally suited to mass-production. The loose-fitting styles were easy to cut, construct and size, and fashionable lightweight fabrics such as silk jersey could be simulated in rayon for a fraction of the price. Moreover their neat, pared-down lines and short length made them practical for everyone, whatever their way of life.[30] Ready-made tailored clothing formed

the basis of the wardrobes of Lucile's 'Dorothys', the working-class shop assistants and business girls whom she sometimes addressed in her weekly column in *The Daily Sketch*. Home dressmaking was also important for this income bracket, and the women's pages of the popular press, such as the 'The London Girl's Dress Gossip' in *Woman's Weekly*, were full of handy tips. During the 1920s the growth in the number of female clerks slowed down, but they still made up 43% of the profession in 1931. Two thirds were under twenty-five, creating a large group of young consumers with money to spend. The average weekly wage for seventeen to twenty year olds was £1. 10s rising to £2 for twenty- to twenty-five-year-olds.[31] These girls could afford to pay 2s. 6d., to dance at the Opera House or Hammersmith Palais and a new summer frock for a night out on the Thames upriver at Taggs Island.[32] The Hon. Mrs C.W. Forester, fashion correspondent of the *Daily Telegraph*, saw the increased access to fashion created by ready-made clothing as a positive force. It generated jobs in the clothing and textile industries, offered women of all classes a creative outlet and enabled the businesswoman to present herself as a professional in the competitive world of work.[33]

As the feminist Mary Stocks remarked: 'We have evolved a type of clothing which is not merely hygienic but also democratic. Never before has it been so difficult to distinguish a factory girl from the unoccupied daughter of an urban landowner.'[34] The homogeneity of mass-produced clothing did not, however, appeal to all London's working girls. For the flappers and their boyfriends, eating alongside hundreds of others in the 'light, co-operative luxury' of Lyons' Strand Corner House, the clothes lacked individuality:

> These great crowds of young people with a little money in their pocket and much zest in their hearts tend to fall into uniform types. The men nearly all buy their collars at the Regent Street branches of City hosiers; the girls seem to skim the lighter froth of the big West End stores, except that Marshall's knows them not. This produces a uniform quality: they have to overtake the fashions, and so become a little *outrées*. [35]

Fig. 89   *Mabs Fashions*, October 1927. The issue included a pattern for a 'trim little frock . . . ideal for the business girl'. (Courtesy of London College of Fashion, University of the Arts London).

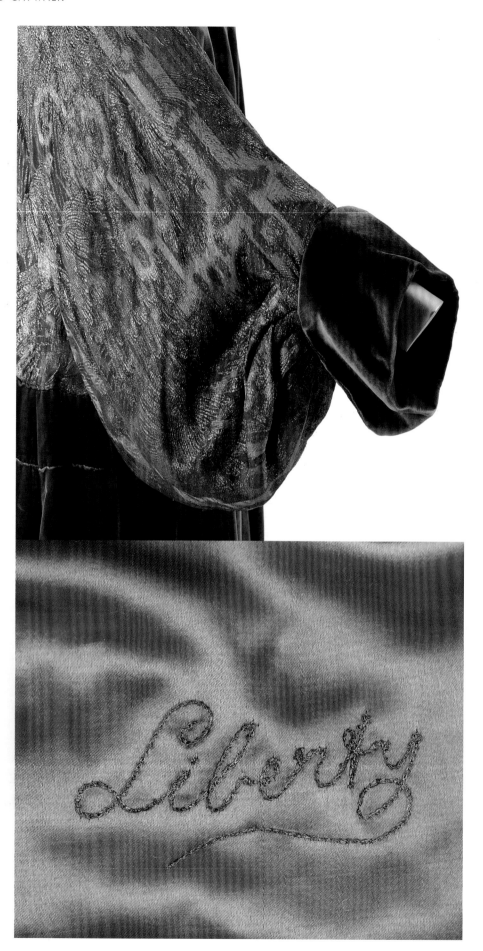

Fig. 90 a, b, and c   Liberty evening
coat with slashed sleeves, c.1929. Made
of silk velvet and brocade.

As with the mid-Victorian 'gents' (see Chapter Two), fashion outdid itself, and the impulse to burlesque mainstream taste can be seen to typify a particular style of metropolitan dressing.

ARTISTIC DRESSING

If Selfridge's epitomised the Americanisation of London, Liberty's was the antidote. Its 1924 'Tudor' extension on Great Marlborough Street self-consciously took the consumer back to a golden age in England's history:

> Here, however, we are face to face with what our ancestors in Tudor days must have known. Not that they had anything like the amplitude in their shops or the variety in their contents that confronts our astonished eyes when we wander about the innumerable galleries and halls of this – I was going to write 'store' – but no one could possibly apply that name to Liberty's. It would be an anachronism; for this building must surely, one thinks, have been standing long before the Pilgrim Fathers adventured on their perilous voyage; long before the New World was called in to purchase the products of the Old ... [36]

Tradition was integral to Liberty's image. The fashions of the 1920s might seem at odds with the concept of tradition, but the vogue for jazz fabrics and snappy sports clothes was balanced by a continuing love affair with the styles, fabrics and decorative motifs of the East that Liberty's was perfectly placed to fulfil. The firm's designers drew on the company's fabric and embroidery archives to create fashionable garments with the Liberty look (fig. 90).

Fig. 91   Silk shawl, 1927–8. Hand-painted by Gwen Pike who worked with Elspeth Little at the Footprints workshop at Durham Wharf, Hammersmith before Little set up Modern Textiles. Pike was a graduate of the Birmingham School of Art.

Fig. 92   Men's fashions from the *Gentlemen's Report of Fashion: What to Wear – and When* by H. M. Dain, *c.*1922. Dain was the proprietor of Burch's, a tailor and breeches maker, at 401 Strand, London.

They also continued to produce more 'artistic', alternative clothes rooted in the aesthetic styles of the nineteenth century. In 1925 Liberty's 'Costumes Never Out Of Fashion' included an Empire line dress with hanging medieval sleeves, a smocked day dress and velvet Stuart gown, which had first appeared as a tea gown in 1908.[37] To add to the time machine effect, Liberty's shopwalkers wore 'medieval' velvet dresses decorated with mock lacing on the sleeves and an embroidered mock girdle.[38] These costumes appealed to older women, intellectuals and artists. Wealthy women seeking artistic clothes with a gloss of modernity patronised Dove in Bond Street. It sold bridge coats, 'smoking dresses' and lounging pyjamas made from antique and modern Oriental fabrics and embroideries alongside luxurious leather driving coats and 'sports kits'. The exotic model Sumurun, 'the Enchantress of the Dessert', who worked for Lucile and Molyneux in Paris, modelled Dove's clothes in 1925.[39]

By the mid-1920s, the revival of interest in craft prompted a fashion for garments and accessories made from block-printed, painted and resist-dyed fabrics. They could be bought from stores such as Liberty's and Marshall & Snelgrove, from artists' studios, at events such as the annual Englishwoman Exhibition and from specialist shops. Kensington's Three Shields Gallery, Modern Textiles in Beauchamp Place and the Little Gallery off Sloane Street catered to a discerning audience who could afford the high cost of an original, hand-made piece: 'Mass production is doubtless very advisable, especially for automobiles, but there will always be people, at least in this country, who prefer to possess something individual rather than something cheap, and it is for them that *Modern Textiles* is opening its modest door.'[40] Significantly their clients included the fashionable interior decorators Syrie Maugham and the New York-based Elsie de Woolf. Many of those involved in the craft movement – whether as artist-designers, practitioners or retailers –

had links with the Slade School of Art, Central School of Arts and Crafts and Royal College of Art. Elspeth Little's Modern Textiles sold fashion fabrics and accessories made by herself, Barron & Larcher, Gwen Pike (fig. 91) and the American-born Marion Dorn. These were displayed alongside simple ready-made garments, furnishing fabric, pottery, glass and sculpture, hangings, rugs and wallpaper.

POSTSCRIPT: MENSWEAR

The emphasis on womenswear in this chapter reflects the new opportunities for education and employment which women enjoyed in the 1920s and their growing independence and purchasing power. Menswear and the tailoring trade remained an important London industry (fig. 92) and there was a 'limited but valuable export trade' in the best London-made clothes.[41] Savile Row and St James's still provided the upper-class London male with all the requirements of his wardrobe and dressing room.

But tastes were changing. Young men in particular wanted to wear more comfortable, practical and less formal clothes even in town. They found a champion in the Prince of Wales whose high profile and passion for clothes made him, like his grandfather King Edward VII, a natural style-leader. The prince found conventional male dress irksome, dull and oppressive. He favoured looser clothes and bright colours, and was quick to adopt new fashions such as the double-breasted dinner jacket introduced to London by American bandleaders.

Fig. 93 *At the Cinema*, 1928. Block print by Grace Golden (1904–92). The figure on the screen is loosely based on Valentino in *The Sheik*.

The casual 'soft' clothes the prince favoured were identified with the United States of America, which was perceived to be taking over every aspect of life in London, from its transport system and the appearance of its streets to the capital's entertainment industry. Film was particularly seductive and its power to influence dress and appearance (fig. 93), like the theatre and music hall that preceded it, was universally acknowledged:

> London has become a city of cinemas. Greta Garbo and Marlene Dietrich reign together, and their names, flashing in many coloured lights, are the only jewels that gleam amid the tatters of the poorer quarters. In the centre of the town they are so close together that they form nothing but a nebulous blazing mass. In the suburbs they bring a little light into the sad streets.[42]

Valentino may have bought his shoes in Mayfair, but his influence spread to the heart of London's East End. The fashion for Valentino hats worn with flashily cut reefer jackets and Oxford bags, noted in Chinatown by Victor Macclure in his 1926 guide to London, demonstrates both the power of the silver screen and the ceaseless and unpredictable fusion of cultures so characteristic of London style.[43]

BROKEN TRADITIONS: 1930–55   *Edwina Ehrman*

The 1930s began on a sombre note. The collapse of America's economy following the Wall Street crash in October 1929 triggered a global financial crisis. International trade declined and markets shrank. In Britain unemployment soared, bringing privation, industrial strife and political instability (fig. 95). Every sector of society was affected. In the City of London many workers were placed on a three-day week and the well-off were forced to retrench. Falling prices and reduced consumer spending affected all levels of London's fashion and clothing trades. Exports decreased and, in the West End there was a noticeable drop in overseas visitors. 'National Economy' was the order of the day and the government urged consumers to 'Buy British'. This was an opportunity London's couturiers could not afford to lose and they wisely built on the city's reputation for fine tailoring and quality sportswear made in British fabrics. They targeted the domestic market, designing:

> for the very practical life of Englishwomen, as opposed to the more luxurious existence led by that limited section of society, the cosmopolitan … Consequently the London dress collections show many tweeds, suits for town and country, dresses with short capes or three-quarter coats, little dresses in fine wool or heavy crêpe or tie silk, the simpler dressmaker suit; and not so many of the ultra formal afternoon-dress or ensemble that Paris delights in.[1]

Norman Hartnell, whose customer profile was more sophisticated and international in outlook, was one of the few designers to show formal afternoon clothes in 1931.

Fig. 94 (*facing*)   Detail of fig. 114, hand-painted silk satin ballgown, 1948. Designed by Norman Hartnell.

Fig. 95 (*left*)   Unemployed girls queuing for work in Farringdon Street, London 17 March 1931. (Fox Photos, Hulton Archive).

Fig. 96 Double-breasted lounge suit, c.1939. Made by Needham & Son of Coram Street, Southampton Row for Max Beerbohm.

Fig. 97 Camel hair overcoat, 1936. Custom-made for John Hartopp by Austin Reed of Regent Street, London.

SAVILE ROW

If London's womenswear designers had grounds for cautious optimism the bespoke menswear trade was less sanguine. Many tailors had suffered from competition from the ready-to-wear trade before the slump, which raised new concerns that the call for economy might encourage the already marked trend towards informality.[2] The start of the London season in 1931 coincided with Budget day and the financial pressures on the country were reflected in the appearance of the crowd attending the first night of the opera, which was traditionally a glittering, formal occasion:

> Tweed overcoats and shabby raincoats were worn over evening dress, even by those who rolled up in sumptuous cars. In some instances hard felt hats usurped the place of ceremonial toppers. Dinner jackets were much too common for a great social event. There were weedy ties and seedy boots. Indeed quite half the men were clad more appropriately for the cinema than grand opera.[3]

The acceptability of 'the suit' for all but the most formal events also threatened sales (fig. 96). The frock coat was almost obsolete and there were fewer occasions when a morning coat or full evening dress, and the appropriate overcoat, was essential. Sports clothes too were looser fitting and more casual, with sweaters worn instead of waistcoats.

But if the domestic market was in decline, Savile Row's international reputation for superb craftsmanship and subtle styling remained intact. Its ambassadors were the Prince of Wales and the new aristocracy, film stars like Jack Buchanan and Fred Astaire. The prince's lounge suits were

made with the 'London cut', developed by Frederick Scholte from the method used to cut military tunics. In its earliest form, the jacket was close-fitting, with a high waist and broad shoulders, but the square-shouldered profile was later accentuated with a draped back giving the wearer a lean, athletic appearance. The cut spread to America where the handsome prince was a fashion idol (fig. 98).

The pressure on Savile Row persuaded some firms to break with tradition and advertise their presence on the street. In 1931 Hawkes & Company, one of the most exclusive firms on the Row, sent shock waves through the trade when they removed the wire blind from their window to reveal cloth draped over stands beneath a discreet signboard. The austere display made no real attempt to woo the passer-by, but it was a subtle repositioning which acknowledged that the trade had to change their business practices if they were to compete in the modern world.

Other tailors cultivated the younger generation and Americans. Kilgour & French in Dover Street made 'ultra-modern clothes for the most dashing type of young man'. Lesley & Roberts in George Street catered for the 'man-about-town' and film stars Clark Gable and Gary Cooper. The Savile Row tailor and trouser specialist Anderson & Sheppard, who favoured 'a rather more cosy and less formal style', numbered the Prince of Wales and Fred Astaire among their clients.[4] London's exclusive men's outfitters were less wary than tailors of engaging with marketplace. Hawes & Curtis in Jermyn Street, who were also patronised by the prince, advertised regularly in *Vogue*. The copy was aimed at women buying gifts for men, but some purchased dressing gowns, pyjamas and shirts for themselves.[5]

Fig. 98   The Prince of Wales, later King Edward VIII, with his brother Prince George on tour in America, 1927. (Hulton Archive).

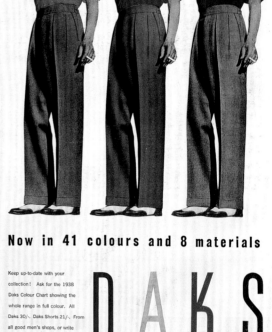

Now in 41 colours and 8 materials

Keep up-to-date with your collection! Ask for the 1938 Daks Colour Chart showing the whole range in full colour. All Daks 30/-. Daks Shorts 21/-. From all good men's shops, or write Simpson, 202, Piccadilly, London.

DAKS

INNOVATORS

The bespoke trade must have watched Austin Reed closely when he moved into ready-to-wear tailoring in 1926. Working with John Barran, one of the largest and most progressive ready-made menswear manufacturers in Leeds, Reed developed a range of fashionable, well-made garments that combined a wide choice of high-quality fabrics with over a hundred fittings.[6] Persuading his middle-class customers to wear 'The New Tailoring' proved a challenge. It took time and money to dissociate it from the dull off-the-peg clothing made for the mass-market in a restricted number of styles, materials and sizes. As committed as ever to the power of advertising (see Chapter Four), Reed launched the range with posters drawn by Tom Purvis which combined a strong image with minimal text. A typical example, advertising business suits in grey pin-head worsted at five and six guineas, depicted a well-dressed commuter at a railway booking office, persuasively associating the man's confident, professional appearance with the New Tailoring.

Austin Reed had made his name as a men's outfitter and shirt specialist catering for City commuters and white-collar workers. As his business expanded, he became more ambitious. In 1923 he moved the company's offices and warehousing from Hackney to an imposing fireproof building in Red Lion Square which was designed on modern functional lines by the architects Percy Westwood and Joseph Emberton. It was christened Summit House after Reed's highly successful Summit brand collars and shirts. Two years later, inspired by a tour of North American department stores, he took advantage of the redevelopment of Regent Street to rebuild and expand his premises to create a department store solely for men. It opened in 1926 stocked with the New Tailoring, and was so successful that Reed soon added to the property.

The shop balanced modernity with tradition and nostalgia, high standards of customer service with a more psychological approach to selling. The interior, designed by Percy Westwood and his sons, took the shopper on an imaginative journey through time and space, distancing him from the hurly-burly of the modern city. Moving from the art deco entrance hall, Reed's customer could visit a fitter in the Louis XV room to order a bespoke shirt or linger in the Liberty-influenced, oak-panelled Tudor galleries where traditional English sportswear, country clothing and rainwear were displayed. Expatriates serving in the empire could find all their needs in the Red Lacquer room, reassured that the man in charge of the tropical department had spent 'twenty years East of Suez'. The room was decorated with eastern furniture, lacquer panels and murals of

Fig. 100   Tailors in Simpson's Stoke Newington factory, early 1930s. (Copyright DAKS Simpson Ltd).

Fig. 101   Classic DAKS, 1936. (Copyright DAKS Simpson Ltd).

ceremonial life in India and Africa by the painter Fred Taylor. The latter showed the Prince of Wales decked out in tropical white receiving the chieftains of West Africa in 1925. The murals reflected the official representation of the empire as Britain's family, united with the mother country by ties of trade and wealth, which was so effectively promoted at the British Empire Exhibition at Wembley in 1924. Finally those in need of relaxation and refreshment could withdraw to the twenty-four-chair barber's shop on the lower ground floor, which was lit like a cocktail bar by a serpentine neon tube and fitted out with baths and showers. 'The scheme of decoration is calculated to soothe and inspire the normal male who hates shopping, and the dominating idea in planning it was to provide in every department the right environment for the particular clothes that can be bought there'. The décor was also designed to engage and flatter the customer and increase his sense of importance by reassuring him of the strength of Britain's traditions and the economic might of her empire.[1]

Reed's Regent Street shop set new standards in menswear retailing, but within ten years of its opening his achievement was challenged by one of the leading wholesale bespoke and ready-to-wear manufacturers, S. Simpson Ltd. Alec Simpson, who became managing director on his father's death in 1932, was known as an innovator. Together with his father, he planned the purpose-built, steel-framed factory housing the firm's workrooms, offices and showrooms in Stoke Newington, which created new standards for the trade. The spacious, well-ventilated workrooms, lit with natural and artificial light, were hygienic and functional, and designed so that the tailors could work in the traditional manner seated on tables (fig. 97). He also invented the DAKS sports trouser, whose self-supporting adjustable waistband did away with the need for braces or belt (the name merged the words DAD and SLACKS). They were exhibited at the British Industries Fair in 1934 in a novel display which was a publicity coup for Simpson and his advertising agency, W. S. Crawford. Instead of using shop mannequins, male models were hired to show Simpson sportswear in action, miming the appropriate movements in front of sets representing a range of sports from golf to sailing.[8] At thirty shillings for trousers and a guinea for shorts, DAKS were expensive but lived up to the brand's catchphrase 'Comfort in Action'. By 1936 they were available in forty-one colours and eight materials (fig. 98).

Fig. 99   Simpson's, 1936. (Copyright DAKS Simpson Ltd).

When Alec Simpson conceived the idea of a central London store, he was determined to create something more modern and more impressive than Austin Reed. 'We are going to identify Simpson clothes in the minds of all men with west end standards of quality and cut, by opening the greatest men's wear store in the west end.'[9] The site he secured between Piccadilly and Jermyn Street suited his aims. It was situated at the heart of London's elite menswear district and was surrounded by tradition and history. On the other side of Piccadilly were the Albany, Burlington House and Burlington Arcade:

> ...the centre of trade in ties and silk card-cases, in club and regimental colours. Opposite, a dealer in skins displays the lovely remains of tigers, the spoils of big rhinoceros and crocodile hunts, and Zululand zebras which people use for interior decoration. Not far from there the grocer Fortnum & Mason ...compose symphonies in hams black as earthenware ...Their neighbour is Hatchard's, a bookshop with a great reputation which has been selling rare books since 1797 in the shadow of St James's Church, built by Wren – On either side of the church are the Royal Watercolour Society ...and the Museum of Geology, which latter adjoins a Lyons's Café that is one of the most unsightly objects in town.[10]

It was on the site of the Museum of Geology that Alec Simpson was to build London's most modern department store which opened on 29 April 1936.

The creation of Simpson Piccadilly brought together a group of exceptionally talented individuals, all of whom were sympathetic to or involved in the modern movement. These included the advertising pioneer W.S. Crawford, his art director Ashley Havinden, architect Joseph Emberton and artist, photographer and filmmaker László Moholy-Nagy, who had been a teacher at the Bauhaus School. He had come to London via Amsterdam in 1935 after fleeing Nazi Germany. Another contributor to Simpson's image of modernity was the Austrian artist and designer Max Hoff, whom Crawford brought to Britain after Hitler annexed Austria in 1938. Havinden's and Hoff's drawings of suave, relaxed, athletic men wearing Simpson clothes, which featured in their advertisements for a quarter of a century, created a strong identity for the firm (fig. 100).

Simpson's introduced a new concept of shopping to London. It assimilated ideas from the United States of America and Europe offering stock sourced in Britain and America in an environment which used the latest technology. Emberton's plans for Simpson's were influenced by the

Fig. 100   Simpson's catalogue, 1938. (Copyright DAKS Simpson Ltd).

Schocken department stores in Germany designed by Erich Mendelsohn and European ideas influenced the store's layout and displays. The floors were not subdivided, creating a spacious, unhurried environment imaginatively lit with natural and artificial light. Large abstract rugs designed by Ashley Havinden and handwoven by the Royal Wilton Carpet Company emphasised the openness of the layout (fig. 99).[11] The stock was housed in wardrobe units veneered with natural wood which provided a foil for blocks of bright colour integrated into the island displays. Jackets and shirts were displayed on heat-formed transparent plastic shapes invented by Moholy-Nagy who was employed as a design consultant to arrange some internal displays and the windows. His displays were functional and appropriate. 'Glamorous flamboyant fittings and décor are not necessary to sell English clothes. They sell on their own merits. That is why I have displayed Simpson's clothes against a plain background that harmonises with them'.[12] The shop also offered bespoke tailoring made in a glazed workroom within the shop, so that customers could watch the tailors at work. This novel arrangement underlined the functionalism of the building and the difference between Simpson and the Savile Row establishments it rivalled. Simpson was a modern business, one that valued transparency and democracy above exclusivity and privilege. Tragically Alec Simpson died within a year of the store's opening aged only thirty-four. Two months later, the women's shop he had planned opened on the fourth floor, selling town and country clothes and DAKS slacks and trouser suits.

EAST END STYLE

For those who had seen New York's Times Square or Friedrichstrasse in Berlin, the coruscating neon advertisements which performed a never-ending show over Piccadilly Circus seemed tame. But no one could deny that London had been transformed by electric light. 'It shines. It is a proud and burnished London, dressed for social life. Throughout its centre it offers white avenues, all of light, and elsewhere are caverns and recesses of gold and diamond. Even the roofs, which once met the upper darkness in an invisible smudge, are now defined in sharp relief.' [13] Light spilled out of shop windows, tempting the passer-by to pause. Stores like Selfridge's and Simpson, which used light as an architectural feature, became landmarks at night. The huge columns outside Selfridge's had been floodlit since 1921, but in 1929 an illuminated art deco canopy designed by Edgar Brandt was erected over the main Oxford Street entrance. Emberton's external illumination of Simpson was more ambitious. Integral to the building's façade, it incorporated 'Cleora Triple Tube Lighting', a British invention first exhibited in 1936 at the Brussels Exhibition. The red, blue and green neon tubes were lit in rotation to create different colours,

Figs. 103, 104   Two-tone men's Oxford shoes, 1925–36 (left). 'Oral' brown suede men's shoes, 1935–9 (right). Oral brand shoes were made by C. W. Horrell of Rushden in Northamptonshire. Unsold stock from Rose, 52 Middlesex Street, Aldgate, London.

and then simultaneously to create bright white light. They were fixed in troughs beneath the panels of Portland stone to shine down on the windows below, creating a magical light show and advertising the pleasure dome of consumption within. [14]

The lights in the East End were more scattered but equally important to the area's social life. Reflecting on the effects of the slump in the East End the writer G. W. Stonier recalled the 'jauntiness' of the young, especially at night as they defied the hard times. 'The promenade from Whitechapel to Mile End was always gayer than Piccadilly. Crowds circled about the few vividly lit pavements and steam trickled down the windows of favourite pubs'.[15] Nor did the Depression stop young people taking an interest in fashion to articulate their youth and independence. Gladys Gibson, an Inspector for the Unemployed Assistance Board, remembered how young tailoresses in Stepney, who had a professional as well as a personal interest in looking smart, purchased fashionable clothes by instalments and bought a stocking a week for sixpence.[16] Family members helped to adapt jumble sale purchases and charitable cast-offs and to make clothes with material bought from markets and cheap department stores. Selfridge's Bargain Basement targeted customers looking for discounts, offering the opportunities of the street market without the haggling and backchat:

> Frocks, seconds, out-sizes, extra shorts, bankrupt stocks . . . Packed files of them dangling from the rigid shoulders of the dress-hangers . . . There are the counters of hats, graded according to price. Housewives trying on hats roll their eyes aslant, while thoughtful friends suck their teeth critically . . . Here's another line of tempting legs, stockings again. Seconds. Flesh-coloured woolly ones at one shilling the pair.[17]

Many women patronised local dressmakers who worked from home or ran small businesses. Lilian Lipley had a shop in Roman Road, Bethnal Green, where she designed ready-made and made-to-measure clothes for customers who included the wives of publicans and members of the Masonic Society, to which her own husband belonged. He was a tailor in Bethnal Green and she had trained as a dressmaker with a West End house where she worked until her marriage. She opened the shop in 1922 and later expanded the premises, building a small workshop in the garden where she employed about ten local women. Several dresses, which Mrs Lipley is thought to have worn herself, have survived. Two evening dresses in the collection of the Museum of London are cut in glamorous, figure-hugging styles in fashionable man-made fabrics (fig. 106).[18] Celia Wilmot, who worked as a secretary in Fleet Street and whose father had been a printworker, paid girlfriends who were milliners and dressmakers to make her best clothes:

Fig. 105   Suede shoes with 11.5cm heels, 1937–9. Made in the East End of London. Unsold stock from Rose, 52 Middlesex Street, Aldgate, London.

> We'd get them to make us a hat, and it was really something unusual, or they would make our dresses for us, and they could make the dresses for a mere ten shillings . . . Oh, I was keen on clothes, very, very keen on dresses . . . As a young girl, basically, one considers one ought to be smart. One would buy a black suit with a check colour, and then you would get a white flat hat with a black-and-white ribbon round it, match it all up. And you'd have your white gloves and your black-and-white shoes, or your black shoes, but you would, on occasions, you would be smart. But you only wore them on Sundays to start off with . . . and you only went out shopping just before Whitsun and just before Christmas – twice a year . . . I even changed my bag to make the colours correct.[19]

'Garish' frocks, 'guaranteed to turn any girl into a good imitation of a movie heroine at fifty yards' could be bought at the Caledonian Market.[20] Better-made but equally standardised versions were sold in the small, individually owned 'madam' shops in Shaftesbury Avenue and Wardour Street in the heart of the West End's entertainment district. The appearance and language of film stars also influenced men. Some commentators

regretted this, associating the Americanisation of London through film with the disappearance of Cockney slang and theatrical London types like the swell. For Thomas Burke, for instance, the gigolo was no replacement.[21] *The Tailor & Cutter* disagreed, recognising commercial possibilities in the weekly exposure of young men and their girlfriends to 'shapely and well favoured men clad in elegant manner'.[22] The professional and social importance of dressing correctly sometimes formed part of a film's plot. In *Behind Office Doors*, which starred Mary Astor as a business girl and Robert Ames as a salesman, his career is transformed as she educates his tastes. *The Tailor & Cutter*, whose readership included suburban as well as West End tailors, ran a weekly feature on the latest films, which included detailed descriptions of the clothes worn by the stars as well as their sartorial *faux pas*, and tailors and outfitters responded by advertising in the free magazines distributed by local cinema chains.[23]

Fig. 106   Rayon crêpe dress, *c.*1933. Made and probably worn by Mrs Lipley.

COUTURE AND THE TIMES

Fig. 107   Custom made three-piece suit, *c.*1935. The subtle use of stripes is typical of several London designers in the 1930s, including Peter Russell and Victor Stiebel.

Fig. 108   Fur-trimmed tweed coat, *c.*1930. Made by W.W. Reville-Terry Ltd, 50 Grosvenor Street, London.

London couture flourished in the 1930s (fig. 107). It was revitalised by a group of talented young designers with common ambitions and sympathetic styles. Digby Morton, an Irishman who designed for Lachasse before setting up his own house in 1933, reformulated the suit, creating a versatile and feminine garment chic enough to wear in London, but sufficiently sporty and understated for smart country events. Hardy Amies, who succeeded him at Lachasse, followed his lead and was rewarded by export orders from America, their common goal. Amies used traditional British woollen fabrics superbly well and his facility with colour and pattern injected wit and novelty into his designs. Peter Russell, like Amies, had no formal training in design; he specialised in beautifully made, well-balanced tailored clothes and sensuous evening wear. Overall, these designers created an identifiable London look based on impeccable tailoring and elegant evening wear. Cecil Beaton photographed their designs against romantic rustic backgrounds or under ballroom chandeliers and their group identity was reinforced by features in *Vogue*, including one illustrated by Francis Marshall showing the designers at work in their studios.[24] Under their direction tailoring became more sensitive to fashion change.

Peter Russell and Victor Stiebel (fig. 109), who grew up in South Africa, had premises in Bruton Street. Stiebel's early life echoed their neighbour Norman Hartnell. Both had briefly read architecture at Cambridge and cut their teeth designing costume and sets for Footlights, but Stiebel trained as a designer at Reville Ltd (fig. 108) before setting up his own house in 1932. His experience at Reville, which was a traditional court dressmaker, gave him an insight into English social customs and the etiquette of dress for the formal royal occasions that were still at the heart of the London social season (fig. 109). Stiebel's fresh, imaginative use of stripes and his romantic evening gowns which blended innocence and sophistication were a perfect choice for debutantes. In 1932 he designed a court presentation dress for Ruth Taylor. The ice-white 'angel-skin' jersey dress, trimmed with piqué flowers and finished with an aquamarine satin train, undoubtedly flattered its wearer. Its colours were calculated to stand out against the rich decoration of the red and gold throne room where the centuries-old ceremony took place. [25] Royal patronage had guaranteed Hartnell's position as London's premier couturier, but he recognised a rival in Stiebel, tartly remarking that he sold clothes 'rather like mine, only more cheaply'.[26]

Britain declared war on Germany in September 1939. London's couturiers continued to ply their craft despite the changed circumstances. The officer's pockets on Digby Morton's suits reflected the military styling which had been creeping into women's clothes, but they also added a fashionable fullness to the hips. Hardy Amies joined the Intelligence Corps and Victor Stiebel enlisted with Army Camouflage, but both maintained a commercial presence in London and designed for projects that fed into the war effort. With the onset of the blitz in September 1940, clothes became more important than fashion. Air raids occurred day and night and the public shelters were overcrowded and squalid (fig. 111). Some families, particularly in the East End which took the brunt of the early raids, lost everything. Large numbers of women of all classes joined the armed forces or took on jobs formerly held by men, whilst others worked in hospitals or did voluntary work. Rosemary Black, a well-off widow with two young children living in St John's Wood, had enrolled as a Mass-Observation recorder, but pleaded for war work after seeing the devastation in the West End and the appalling conditions at Piccadilly underground station. In Oxford Street, John Lewis' department store was:

> the most ghastly sight imaginable. I had no notion that the empty, charred skeleton with its blackened walls and gaping windows and rust-orange girders and its wax models lying like corpses on the pavement could look so terrible and forbidding. The pictures in the papers had given no idea of the appalling reality ... HORRIFIED by ghastly sights in Tubes ... The misery of that vast wretched mass of humanity sleeping like worms in a packed tin – the heat and smell, the dirt, the endless crying of the poor bloody babies, the haggard white-faced women nursing their children against them, the children cramped and twitching in their airless, noisy sleep. Even a disused escalator was crowded with dumb, resigned humanity ... [27]

The cost of clothing rose rapidly between 1939 and 1941, prompting the Board of Trade to introduce a raft of measures controlling the supply of cloth, clothing and footwear. They included clothes rationing in June 1941, the Utility scheme, which controlled the quality and price of Utility cloth and clothing, and, from the spring of 1942, the Civilian Clothing (Restriction) Orders, which imposed stringent austerity regulations governing the construction, materials and trimming of nearly every item of clothing whether made in a couture house or factory (fig. 112). Their purpose was to keep prices down, make the most appropriate and economical use of scarce raw materials and ensure a fair distribution of clothing to all. [28] At the same time

the government encouraged people to 'make do and mend'. Hats and headscarves were coupon-free. For those who could afford them, they were a morale-boosting tonic, introducing a little frivolity, self-indulgence and personal style into their diminishing wardrobes (fig. 110). Headscarves printed with patriotic slogans and motifs were particularly popular. The fabric and fashion house Jacqmar, with which Victor Stiebel and Bianca Mosca were associated during the war, made a speciality of them.

Austerity regulations were introduced in 1942 to save material and labour and increase production. To dispel any suggestion that they would lead to standardisation, the Board of Trade drew on the expertise of London's couturiers. Guaranteeing anonymity, they commissioned designs for a basic non-seasonal wardrobe of a coat, suit and blouse or shirt, and a day dress suitable for mass-manufacture. The designs were well-cut, smart and practical but their styling could look retrospective. They conformed to the board's demand that the clothes should be desirable, but not so new that they overstimulated demand.[29] For their part, the designers argued that the same fabric savings could be made, with less red tape, by simply restricting yardage.[30] Over a hundred manufacturers placed orders for templates of the thirty-two designs and in October, *The*

Fig. 109 a, b and c (*facing*)   Full-length wool evening coat, c.1936. Designed by Victor Stiebel and embellished with raised metal thread embroidery.

Fig. 110 (*above*)   Rayon linen headscarf, 1945. Purchased by the London Museum from Bourne & Hollingsworth immediately after the war ended. Clothes rationing was not abolished until 1949.

Fig. 111   East End Underground
station shelter, 12 November 1940.
Photograph by Bill Brandt (1904–83).
(The Imperial War Museum).

Illustrated London News ran a feature showing the prototypes, which the Board of Trade donated to the Victoria & Albert Museum, alongside factory-made copies which compared favourably with the originals.[31] The tight control of textile and clothing manufacture during the war improved manufacturing and production standards. It was also generally agreed that the challenge of designing within the regulations had a positive effect on factory-made clothing, which in turn educated public taste.

The designers who worked with the Board of Trade belonged to the Incorporated Society of London Fashion Designers. The society, always known as Inc. Soc., was founded in January 1942 to

Fig. 112   Herringbone weave wool austerity dress, *c.*1944. Made with six seams in the skirt and four buttons, the maximum number allowed. The lap seam on the bodice is not a tuck, which was not allowed, but a constructional join. Otto Marcus, a clothing manufacturer in Wells Street, donated the dress to the London Museum.

Fig. 113   Woman's wooden-soled suede walking shoes, *c.*1944. Made according to the austerity regulations. Wooden soles were introduced to save leather, although they had to be protected by leather or rubber studding. They remained unpopular until the coupon value was reduced to two.

promote and support the interests of London couture, which, unlike Paris couture, had no official representative body. Several members had previously belonged to the Fashion Group of Great Britain, whose primary aim had been to develop sales in the United States. The government backed the society from the outset, recognising its export potential and the organisational advantages of working with a single group. Members in 1942 included Edward Molyneux, Charles Creed and Bianca Mosca (who came to London after the occupation of Paris), Norman Hartnell (fig. 114), Hardy Amies, Digby Morton, Peter Russell, Victor Stiebel and Worth of London. Throughout the 1940s and 50s, glossy magazines such as *Vogue* and *Harper's Bazaar* energetically promoted the group, but the daily press was more sceptical. In 1950, Edna McKenna dubbed the group the 'Timorous Ten': 'Very wearable – yes. But where are all those new ideas?'[32]

France's Chambre Syndicale de la Couture Parisienne had fifty-six members, each employing an average of five hundred staff, with double that number at Dior, who benefited financially from the French government's *aide de la couture* and from their close ties with the French textile industry. In London, Inc. Soc. had twelve members, who were mainly self-financed. The largest employed no more than two hundred and fifty staff. In 1955 the society's president Pamela Berry stated that they owed their success to working within the *status quo* and knowing their market. Accepting that they had neither the authority nor the financial backing to innovate fashions like the elite Paris houses, they tailored their collections to the requirements of the London season, and the tastes (and often limited budgets) of their upper- class clients, creating the kind of elegant, understated, 'well-bred' clothes typical of this small section of British society. The patronage of the royal family increased their prestige and attracted worldwide publicity, generating healthy exports, particularly to the Commonwealth countries such as Australia and Canada which had strong ties with Britain.[33] All this was true but their narrow focus and concentration on wearable, occasion-specific clothes cramped their style and vision. Fashion, particularly in London, was on the cusp of change. The rising generation were not interested in becoming 'professional dressers' with all the time-consuming fittings this entailed. They were less concerned with class and protocol and wanted more adventurous, youthful and sexy fashions that could be bought off the peg and wouldn't last a lifetime.

NEW LOOKS ALL ROUND

Christian Dior's debut collections in 1947 introduced a new model of womanhood. It was an ideal which looked backwards to the graceful, mature, corseted femininity so admired before the First World War. His 'New Look', which reaffirmed Paris's position as the undisputed leader of fashion, was the antithesis of the wartime line which now appeared mean and old-fashioned. The essential elements of the style – a softer shoulder line, nipped-in waist and full hips – were already part of the design repertoire, but the proportions, scale and luxury of the New Look fully justified the epithet. It was impractical, inappropriate to the harsh economic climate, and required unpatriotic amounts of material, but women everywhere were tantalised by its glamour and uninhibited extravagance, and it was new, so the press promoted it as they derided it. The tailored London version, which appeared in 1948, had noticeably wider shoulders and a less constricted waist (fig. 115). It was, characteristically, more practical, but it also had swagger.

Men too were looking for a new image. The adoption of fancy waistcoats by upper-class men in London after the war looked back to the Edwardian period, when luxury was their right and Savile Row unchallenged. The New Edwardians rejected the American-influenced wide-shouldered drape suit in favour of a more fitted style, with natural shoulders and a suppressed waist, worn with increasingly narrow trousers. Jackets and velvet-collared coats buttoned high and combined Edwardian taste with a military styling carried through into turned-back cuffs. The more affected proponents of the style carried canes and wore light-coloured gloves (fig. 116). Norman Parkinson's iconic photograph, 'Back to Formality: Savile Row', which appeared in *Vogue* in April 1950, emphasised its class roots and military overtones. The clever composition, shot against the light to emphasise the new silhouette, featured three immaculately groomed Savile Row habitués, whose burnished shoes and bowlers, starched white collars and immaculately furled umbrella, identified them with upper-crust, elitist values of old England.

Adolescent and young working-class men were also looking for alternative ways of dressing. They wanted clothes that expressed their youth and asserted their independence, both from the establishment and their elders. Some turned to casual, contemporary styles imported from the United States of America and sold in shops like Cecil Gee in Charing Cross Road. They wore drape jackets and American shirts with long pointed collars, wide-brimmed fedoras, windcheaters and baggy trousers. Their manner aped the free and easy ways and language of the American troops whose glamorous presence had reinforced the mania for American popular culture during the war years. Dedicated jive fans wore zoot suits, which were originated by black and Chicano

Fig. 114   Hand-painted silk satin ball-gown with a pink silk underskirt, 1948. Designed by Norman Hartnell. The hips were padded with cotton wadding to achieve the fashionable New Look. The dress was ordered by Hermione Wills to take with her when she emigrated to America.

Fig. 115   Ribbed wool New Look coat, spring 1949. Designed by Hardy Amies.

Fig. 116   'Covert' style topcoat with a panelled velvet collar, 1953. Made by Joce & Company of Albemarle Street, London. Joce won the international Dandy Tailoring Trophy awarded by *The Tailor & Cutter* magazine five times.

Americans in the late 1930s, with drape jackets reaching to the knees, peg trousers and long watch-chains. Their girls wore skimpy pleated swing skirts over tight, short but modest pants. Black G.I.s, mostly in uniform, danced alongside them. Up to 3,000 people attended the Hammersmith Palais on jive nights. But the most groundbreaking venue was the Lyceum; its jive sessions every Friday from midnight until four in the morning opened up London's night life to anybody who could pay the four shillings admission.[34] By 1950, however, the American look had become identified with the shady dealing spiv and a more delinquent gang mentality.

The Teddy boys went one stage further. They appropriated the Edwardian look and mockingly merged it with the American styles that were anathema to its originators. Their flamboyant, overtly sexual style first appeared in the East End and north London and then crossed the river and went west. Teds wore long 'fingertip' draped jackets with velvet collars and cuffs, narrow ties, peg trousers or drainpipe jeans, and brothel creepers (fig. 117). They bought their clothes from local tailors, paying between £15 and £20 for a suit.[35] Their hair expressed their difference as

Fig. 117   Teddy boys in Trafalgar Square, 1953.
Photograph by Henry Grant. (Henry Grant
Collection, Museum of London).

much as their outfits. They grew it long – in stark contrast to the military short back and sides
inflicted on national servicemen – and greased it into a quiff, which they ritually combed in public. By 1953 the press had caught up with them, and there were enough reports of incidents
involving young delinquents wearing 'Edwardian-type' clothes for the tailoring trade to worry
that the original style, which was moving into mainstream tailoring, would be rejected by the man
in the street. The net result, of course, was that both styles became diluted and absorbed into the
mass market, creating a pattern which would be repeated many times as London's vibrant cultural
scene became a breeding ground for alternative styles.

Every decade has its city. During the shell-shocked 1940s thrusting New York led the way, and in the uneasy fifties it was the easy Rome of *La Dolce Vita*. Today it is London, a city steeped in tradition, seized by change, liberated by affluence – in a decade dominated by youth, London has burst into bloom. It swings, it is the scene.[1]

This was how *Time* magazine identified 'swinging London' in 1966: quintessentially cocky and challenging, at the cutting edge, and inherently youthful. The stereotype has stuck. It was in the post-war period that the *idea* of London fashion crystallised, as much through its imagery and media representation as in its actual clothes. Fashion has served as a prism to magnify both the 'swinging London' of the 1960s and the 'Cool Britannia' of the 1990s, even though in reality it is a relatively small industry compared to those of the United States or Italy. Magazines like *Nova* in the 1960s and *i-D* in the 1980s contributed to this youth-oriented culture.[2] Those who propelled London fashion forwards from the late fifties – designers, retailers, journalists, publishers – were from the same generation, and often the same social scene, as their target audiences. They both reflected and generated new fashion, creating a symbiotic relation between producers, consumers and promoters of style. The myth and reality of London fashion may have been completely at odds at times, but the mix has remained a potent and productive one.

Quantum Leaps

The 1960s sum up much that is typical of London fashion. John Cowan's fashion photographs for the *Sunday Times* colour supplement (fig. 118) fuse carefree youth with gritty urban realism, juxtaposing the blond model against the brutalist tower block in a decade when the architecture of London's cityscape changed radically. Yet many of the decade's novelties originated in the late fifties, that bridge between forties austerity and sixties affluence.

British fashion photography entered a new era in the 1950s. Home-grown photographers began to rise alongside the French and Italian ones whose work had previously featured in British magazines. Until the early 1950s, fashion illustration in newspapers tended to be sketches as they reproduced better than photographs. When high-fashion photographs began to appear in mass-circulation newspapers it was due to the London-based photographer John French, who devised new ways of lighting fashion shoots that produced photographs sharp enough for newsprint. His *Daily Express* photographs of the model Barbara Goalen defined the look of the fifties: pencil skirts and jackets with nipped-in waists accessorised with pearls and white gloves. French is also credited with the invention of the bull-dog clip as a styling accessory that sharpened up the silhouette by fitting clothes to the body. Both David Bailey and Terence Donovan (fig. 124), who were to define the look of sixties photography, started as assistants to John French.

Fashion publishing was shaken up in 1957 when the twenty-five-year-old Jocelyn Stevens acquired the society magazine *Queen*. With Mark Boxer as art editor and featuring the photographs of Anthony Armstrong-Jones and Norman Parkinson, its irreverent, witty and youthful style set the pace for many 1960s developments. In the early sixties *Vogue*'s 'Young Ideas' page was an important source of new fashions, and provided crucial coverage that helped establish rising London boutiques. For men, *Man About Town* became a style bible after 1961 under new art direction, first as *About Town* and then simply *Town*.

Fig. 118   Model jumping in front of sixties tower block. Photograph by John Cowan (1929-1979). (Copyright Carolyn Cowan).

Fig. 119   Window display at the Knightsbridge branch of Mary Quant's Bazaar, 1961. (Copyright Mary Quant Ltd).

It was not only magazine layout and content that reflected the shifts of the late 1950s and early sixties, but also modelling. Models in the early fifties had tended to be society girls, who lived in Belgravia service flats and went out with wealthy, upper-class men. Jean Shrimpton, the first of the new wave, started modelling in 1960. The photographs that David Bailey took of her in the three and a half year period of their association defined the look of 'the Shrimp': youthful, leggy, tomboyish, with long tousled hair and pale lipstick. The new look was taken up in the *Sunday Times* colour supplement (started in April 1962) with a front cover by Bailey of Shrimpton in a Mary Quant dress.

Youth, cool and popular culture also defined the London look. A new type of fashion designer emerged, often art-school trained, high-spirited and iconoclastic. This younger generation of designers and retailers worked in ignorance of the established London couture traditions of, say, Hardy Amies and Norman Hartnell. While doing an art and illustration course at Goldsmiths College of Art in the early fifties, Mary Quant met her future husband and business partner Alexander Plunket Greene. His shantung silk pyjama tops worn over his mother's slim-fitting trousers ensured that he stood out from the crowd, as did Quant's equally outlandish short gingham skirts, knee socks and sandals. They opened their first boutique, Bazaar, on the King's Road in 1955 when Quant was twenty-one. By her own account, the young Quant was so ignorant of the protocols of dressmaking that, unaware that she could purchase cloth wholesale, she bought all the material for her earliest designs at Harrod's, and made them up from amended Butterwick paper patterns.[3] Such cheerful chaos and uncommercial lack of forward-planning continue to typify the production methods of many London designers.

The Quant style of the fifties – simple, neat and unfussy, often using cotton gabardine, poplin or gingham – made a direct appeal to a newly emerging youth market. Above all, it made the idea of the very young woman fashionable, rather than the more matronly figures who patronised the Mayfair dressmakers. Accessories and jewellery were sourced from students at the London art schools, or made up overnight. Merchandise often sold out in a day and would be replaced the next morning with new designs made up in Quant's flat, a novel contrast to the strict adherence to seasonal production in the trade.

When Bazaar opened, the King's Road was still a residential high street, though already beginning to be populated by beatniks and coffee bars. Quant wanted, and achieved, arresting window displays that people would cross the street to see. Designed by John Bates (who would later design the clothes for the cult television series *The Avengers*) they were quirky and fast-changing, with mannequins in surreal or jokey poses. Novel window displays also characterized the second Bazaar, which opened in Knightsbridge in 1957 (fig. 119). Quant brought the same iconoclasm to trade shows abroad, where she eschewed the salon tradition of hushed, dignified presentation. Instead, her models danced frenetically to pop music and, being photographic rather than salon models, froze in haughty, dramatic poses on the catwalk.

Quant stood out not only because she was an innovative designer, but also for her style and ethos. Her life with Plunket Greene revolved around modern jazz and coffee bars as much as fashion production, and Bazaar was both a social and a retail space. 'Our friends and acquaintances were painters, photographers, architects, writers, socialites, actors, con-men, and superior tarts,' Quant recalled.[4] This interface of fashion and art, or fashion and pop culture, then became fashionable abroad and was exported successfully as an idea of London fashion. What was true of Quant in the sixties was also the case for Westwood in the eighties and Galliano and McQueen in the nineties.

The newspapers wrote a great deal about the 'Chelsea set'. But according to Quant, it was not a set at all, simply a loose association of creative people from different backgrounds. By the time the press had identified the Chelsea set, its coverage seemed 'rather bogus' and included none of the original participants. As Quant herself recalled, 'Nobody has ever been able to make up his mind precisely what "the Chelsea Set" was but I think it grew out of something in the air which developed into a serious effort to break away from the Establishment,' [5] an idea that had first been mooted in August 1959 when *Queen* magazine's spoof 'The Establishment Chronicle' mocked class, privilege and the London old-boy network in a parody of 'The Eton Chronicle'.

In menswear too, change was in the air. Vince opened in Newburgh Street in the West End in 1954, selling brightly coloured and tightly tailored menswear to the 'theatrical crowd', a synonym for a gay clientele in the days before homosexuality was decriminalised.[6] In 1957 John Stephen opened his shop in nearby Carnaby Street selling mod styles to young men. It was largely due to his influence that by the early sixties Carnaby Street had acquired its reputation for innovative London fashion. In the immediate post-war period, Cecil Gee had transposed the institution of high-quality East End Jewish tailoring to Charing Cross Road where he sold American-look drape suits. By 1959 he had fourteen shops in central London and was selling Italian cotton suits made up in London by a tailor he had brought over from Rome. Though popular with modern jazz fans, the Italian style was generally considered effete and unmanly; in 1956 the singer Frankie Lane appeared at the London Palladium in the Italian look to the horror of the press and, it was claimed, his female fans.[7] Hardy Amies commented on Italian tailors' 'somewhat dubious taste – dubious because there was no real sense of tradition behind them'.[8] With young people, however, style was more important than tradition. In the 1960s the three-button Italian suit morphed into the classic mod suit, with its bum-freezer jacket ideal for riding a Vespa scooter, and Soho tailors made up the suits that Savile Row tailors decried.

This triumph of subcultural style over gentlemanly substance points to the increasing democratisation of London fashion in the post-war period. The late 1950s was a period of high employment. With the consumer boom came new, transatlantic, influences in film, television, magazines and rock and roll. All contributed to the way in which the image of the American teenager was appropriated in Britain in the mid-fifties and early sixties. This produced that much-discussed social phenomenon: the generation gap. These emerging markets generated their own social spaces, the caffs, milk bars and record shops that linked new fashions to the topography of the city and its suburbs. Karel Reisz's 1958 film *The Lambeth Boys* showed working-class Teddy boys in south London's Kennington. And later, in the early seventies, Malcolm McLaren and Vivienne Westwood catered to revival Teds (fig. 120).

As the fifties turned into the sixties, the Moderns emerged. Mods rode scooters and wore lean, slick Continental tailoring. But the look they made their own was quintessentially a London one. According to George Melly, they were 'cool as ice cubes' and used each other as looking glasses.9 Colin MacInnes' 1959 London novel *Absolute Beginners* described the dowdy look of middle-class trad jazz fans and the Neanderthal Ted, who was already lagging behind the times sartorially and musically. MacInnes saves his approval for the Modernist:

> College-boy, smooth crop hair with burned-in parting, neat white Italian rounded-collared shirt, short Roman jacket very tailored (two little vents, three buttons), no-turn-up narrow trousers with 17-inch bottoms absolute maximum, pointed-toed shoes and a white mac lying folded by his side ... Modern jazz boy's girl – short hem-lines, seamless stockings, pointed toe high-heeled stiletto shoes, crêpe nylon rattling petticoat, short blazer jacket, hair done up into the elfin style. Face pale – corpse colour with a dash of mauve, plenty of mascara.10

Set in Notting Hill Gate, *Absolute Beginners* perfectly describes the imperative to be achingly up-to-date, totally modern. Yet the mini-skirted mod girls of 1969 in the suburb of Borehamwood (fig. 121) exemplify the way that the lived experience of subcultures spreads further, both topographically and temporally, than the histories of its vanguard would suggest.11 It is possible that, by 1969, the more modish proto-Mods described by MacInnes might have been experimenting

Fig. 120   Teds outside the Black Raven Pub, Bishopsgate, City of London, *c*.1972. Photograph by Roger Perry.

with the psychedelic styles of the late sixties, before reinventing themselves, yet again, as glam-rockers in the 1970s. The image is also a reminder of the hybrid affiliations that characterised all post-war London subcultures. All white subcultures were also, even if unconsciously, enormously influenced by black styles in the period after the arrival of the ss Windrush in 1948.[12] Immigrants from the Caribbean introduced West Indian styles, which became incorporated in London sub-cultures throughout the 1960s. Just as the rude boy style of ska crossed over musically, so too did the 'sta-prest' trousers, the Crombie overcoat and the pork-pie hat that were, variously, adopted by skinheads and, later, by punks.

In 1965, the now established *Queen* was challenged by a new magazine, *Nova,* which lasted until 1975. Visually innovative, and more concerned with aesthetic breakthroughs than sales, *Nova* had interesting articles on topics of the day. Under the fashion editorship first of the Welsh painter Molly Parkin and, from 1967, the future stylist Caroline Baker, the magazine included an eccentric mix of high fashion, army surplus, plastic and non-fashion items, rather than tradi-tional haute couture. The startling photographs by the likes of Hans Feurer included fat women, old women, and faux-realist sex scenes of a sort that had never before been seen in fashion edito-rials.

Modelling styles shifted too. If Jean Shrimpton had been the quintessential girl of the early six-ties, 1966 saw the overnight success of an even more influential model, the sixteen-year-old

Fig. 121   Gang of Mod youths, Borehamwood, 1969. Photograph by Terry Spencer. (Copyright Terry Spencer).

Fig. 122   'Peachy' dress and hat, 1960.
Tweed shift dress designed with a
matching broad-brimmed hat by Mary
Quant.

Fig. 123   PVC 'Christopher Robin'
raincoat and sou'wester, 1963.
Designed by Mary Quant.

Twiggy. Coming from the London suburb of Neasden, Twiggy's endearingly chirpy and unaffected persona was far removed from the aristocratic demeanour of London models in the 1950s. She had a cockney accent, frank opinions, cropped hair, a tiny frame and long legs. She painted huge mock eyelashes below her eyes. Photographers and editors played up her gamine look, dressing her in skimpy ribbed jumpers and tiny skirts, and putting her in knock-kneed poses. The East End also provided the visual chroniclers for 'up West': the photographers Terence Donovan, David Bailey and Brian Duffy.[13] Yet the so-called classlessness of the sixties was, even in the worlds of fashion and pop, a meritocracy of the young and included a fair share of old Etonian entrepreneurs, not least in the boutiques that sprang up around the King's Road.

Alexandra Pringle remembers young women of Chelsea 'catwalking' up and down the King's Road near Bazaar:

They wore big floppy hats, skinny ribbed sweaters, key-hole dresses, wide hipster belts and, I believe, paper knickers. They had white lipsticked lips and thick black eyeliner, hair cut at alarming angles, op-art earrings and ankle-length white boots. They wore citron-coloured trouser suits and skirts that seemed daily shorter. They rode on miniature motorbikes. They had confidence and, it seemed, no parents.[14]

By 1965 the mini was almost six inches above the knee; it peaked around 1966–7. Credit for the invention of the mini was hotly contested. In London Quant had shown very short skirts briefly in 1961; in Paris in 1964 Courrèges' influential collection featured short skirts, but they were soon overtaken by Quant's. In 1958 she had adapted Givenchy's 1957 sack dress for a London market, and by the mid-sixties it had become the mini shift dress whose shape was to dominate the decade. This two-way trade shows how hawkishly London and Paris designers watched each other, even if they did not acknowledge the other's influence. Foale & Tuffin's sharply cut trouser suits anticipated Yves Saint Laurent's 'le smoking' by several years. The famous round-necked jackets made for the Beatles in 1963 by Dougie Millings, the Old Compton Street 'showbusiness tailor', as the brass nameplate on his door boasted, were like the collarless jackets Pierre Cardin had shown two years earlier in Paris, though Millings added braided edges and other touches. Quite separately, the Modern jazz fan and soon-to-be London retailer Tommy Roberts recalls having one made up in black cord from a Jacques Fath pattern in 1961.[15]

Regardless of who originated it, Quant made the controversial mini-skirt considerably shorter than anyone else, and her clientele of savvy young London girls willingly took to it. Quant's look was epitomised by pinafores in mustard or check, often worn over polo-necked jumpers or white blouses, and accessorised with matching tweedy hats (fig. 122). Her black PVC raincoat (fig. 123)

Fig. 124   Mary Quant, 1963. Photograph by Terence Donovan (1936–96). (Copyright Terence Donovan Archive).

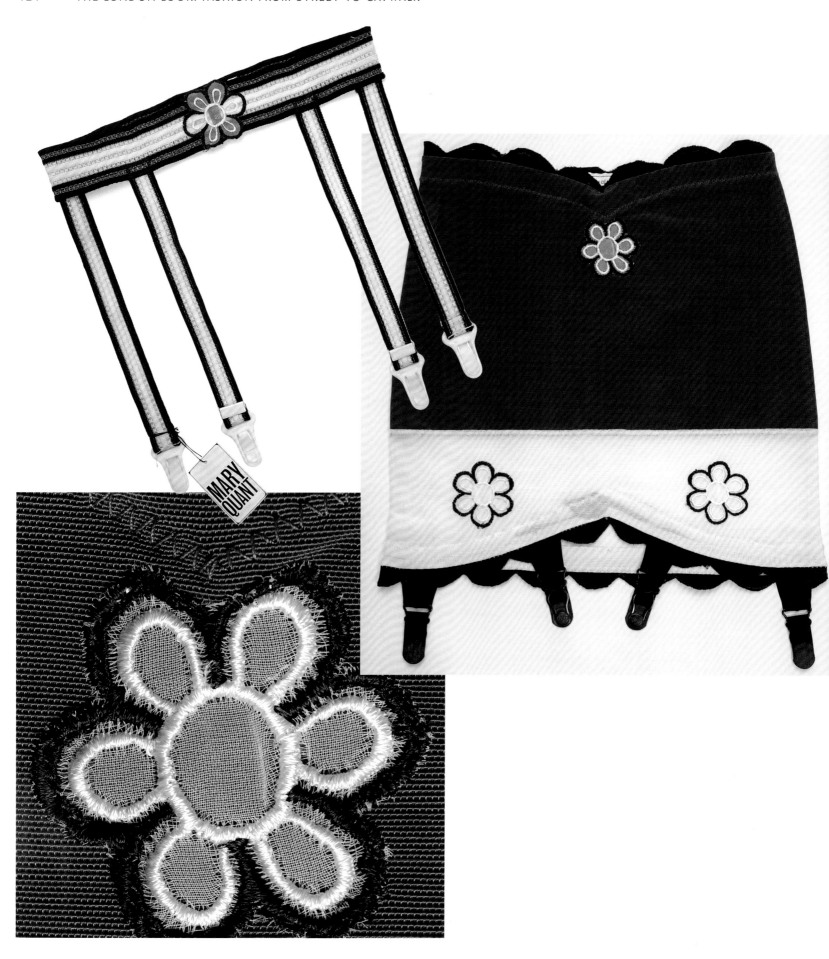

that fastened up the back is typical of her use of the material. The clothes were not particularly cheap, but they were highly desirably all the same. Quant wore hers with the sharp, geometric Vidal Sassoon haircut that not only characterised the look but revolutionised hair cutting and styling (fig. 124).

From outré beginnings, Quant rapidly moved to the fashion mainstream through astute merchandising. She started wholesaling in 1961 and launched the Ginger Group in 1963 to franchise her slightly cheaper designs for mass-manufacture. American deals followed, as did Quant cosmetics and underwear that sported the famous Quant daisy (fig. 125). In 1966 she was awarded an OBE for her services to fashion exports as part of prime minister Harold Wilson's aggressive capitalisation on the pop and fashion cultures of the city. She collected the award in a mini (fig. 126). The heavy gauge of the cream and navy jersey fabric gave the dress structure and presence, while the top stitching, the zip detailing at neck and cuffs, and the suggestion of a sailor's collar when worn unzipped, evoked the casual chic and crisp modernity of the earliest designs of Coco Chanel, but with a distinctly London edge.

Fig. 126 (*above*) Cream wool jersey dress with navy facing at collar and cuffs, 1966. Designed and worn by Mary Quant to collect her OBE from Buckingham Palace.

Fig. 125 a, b and c (*facing*) Mary Quant underwear, 1965. Nylon and lycra mix girdle and suspender belt.

Fig. 127 The pop singer Lulu on the set of *Ready, Steady, Go*, 1964. Photograph by Henry Grant. (Henry Grant Collection, Museum of London).

BIBA AND THE BOUTIQUES

In *The Young Meteors*, Jonathan Aitken wrote: 'The fashion revolution is the most significant influence on the mood and *mores* of the younger generation of the last decade ... Fashion ... binds the entire younger generation with a new sense of identity and vitality. Britain's capital has been given a completely new image at home and abroad.'[16] Aitken may have been referring to the 1966 *Time* feature on 'swinging London', but by the time the myth was cemented as a foreign export, the image at home had already become a little ossified. Carnaby Street had become a tourist site, and fashion cognoscenti turned their attention from new things to old, moving west towards the Portobello Road. A softer, more romantic trend was typified by the Kensington boutique Biba which opened in Abingdon Road in 1964. Alexandra Pringle remembered: 'At the very beginning Biba was a hangout for dollybirds of the Cathy McGowan variety: long fringes and large spikey eyes under hats studded with holes like an Emmenthal cheese, in shifts made from upholstery fabrics.'[17] Every Friday night between 1963 and 1966, live at 6pm, Cathy McGowan presented the pop music television programme *Ready Steady Go* whose introductory countdown '5 – 4 – 3 – 2 – 1' signalled the start of the weekend (fig. 127). The iconic McGowan wore Biba and Foale & Tuffin, but never the same outfit twice. For her London audience, keeping up with what she wore marked the accelerated consumption of sixties style, when boutique shopping offered constantly changing stock.

The brains behind Biba was Barbara Hulanicki who initially sold her designs via mail order, working from home with the help of her husband and mother. The fashion journalist Brigid Keenan described the first shop:

> The tiny boutique they opened sold the same sort of simple, inexpensive clothes, plus some amusing accessories, and soon girls were queuing outside. On busy days, customers were stripping off and trying things on in the street. Barbara and Fitz were forced to move to bigger premises. They and the shop assistants pushed the dress rails hung with clothes along the pavements to their new shop in Kensington Church Street, a colourful informal place with old-fashioned stands full of felt hats and feather boas, and the first communal changing room.[18]

Biba stayed in Kensington Church Street until 1969 when it moved in round the corner to Kensington High Street. In 1971, Lee Bender opened her boutique Bus Stop next door to the old Biba premises, in a shop where bored-looking boyfriends were admitted to the women's communal changing rooms (figs 128, 129). Hulanicki's Biba look was waif-like compared to Quant's robust city girl. The contrast signalled an important shift from a crisp, modern aesthetic to nostalgic dalliance with retro styles: William Morris and Victoriana, Hollywood and the twenties and

Fig. 128   Printed synthetic jersey dress, c.1975. Designed by Lee Bender for Bus Stop.

Fig. 129   Biba gold satin dress with metallic paisley pattern waistcoat, 1969–72.

thirties. With its narrow shoulders and tightly cut upper arms, a Biba outfit suited a narrow frame, a hollow chest, a pale complexion and soulful, highly made-up, large dark eyes. The Biba gold satin mini-dress, with its romantic sleeves and long floppy tie at the neck, worn with a long metallic brocade waistcoat, shows how Quant's mod style could be transformed into a softer image (fig. 129). Within a few years the look had evolved into 'clothes for the sinful and *louche*'; Alexandra Pringle would try on 'slithery gowns in glowing satins, hats with black veils, shoes stacked for sirens' and contemplate 'make-up – chocolate and black – for vamps and vampires'.[19] The look was consolidated in a range of Biba catalogues photographed by Sarah Moon (fig. 130). Moon's influential photographic style both captured the distinctive Biba look and helped Hulanicki break new ground in the mail order business which had never before been used to sell high fashion.

For men, the sixties offered conceivably even greater opportunities for novelty and self-transformation. In the mid-sixties, Carnaby Street and then Chelsea continued to be the principal spaces of male fashion. By about 1966 the Chelsea dandies, in Jon Savage's words, provided a model for pop groups like the Beatles and the Rolling Stones, another way in which London style was exported worldwide.[20] Chelsea dandies wore narrow double-breasted suits that fastened high on the chest, in velvet or regency stripes, with kipper ties or floating scarves. Well into the early

Fig. 130   Biba mail-order catalogue number six, 1969. Photograph by Sarah Moon.

seventies the influence of the King's Road boutiques continued to make itself felt as department stores pioneered in-store versions such as Harrods' Way In and Selfridge's Miss Selfridge.

In 1965 Michael Rainey opened his menswear boutique Hung on You in Chelsea Green, moving to the King's Road in 1967. It closed in 1969 but in that short time it typified the familiar features of London fashion: a 'scene' that was social as much as sartorial, fashion that was extreme and individualistic. Quirky, unconventional clothes sold to a pop and media clientele. Haphazardly made and expensive, but also highly designed, Hung on You clothing was riotous and colourful, featuring lace and bright colours for men and, towards the end of the decade, kaftans. Its chaotic retail system with 'cool' mini-skirted shop assistants who ignored the customers was, again, typical of a certain school of London entrepreneurship.

At World's End, at the end of the King's Road, Nigel Waymouth's Granny Takes a Trip opened in 1966, demonstrating the same entrepreneurial chaos and cool management. It sold a mixture of its own designs and old clothes to both sexes. The look was androgynous, with no attempt to differentiate male and female dress. Everything was displayed on the same rail and tried on in the single, unisex changing room. The atmosphere was intimidating, and it was not intended to be welcoming by its public-school-educated owners, Waymouth and Michael English.[21] In English's mural designs for the shop, fashion, music and graphic art came together in a specifically London mix (fig. 131).

Fig. 131   Façade of Granny Takes a Trip, 488 Kings Road, Chelsea, c. 1967. (Copyright Hulton Deutsch Collection Ltd).

Fig. 132 (*below*)   Bias-cut crêpe-de-chine dress, c. 1973. Designed by Ossie Clark. Print designed by Celia Birtwell.

Fig. 133 (*centre*)   Mr Fish shirt and tie, 1973–6. Transparent black, self-striped, organdie shirt lined over the torso with orange cotton and worn with a colour co-ordinating satin tie. The donor remembered: 'Mr Fish, it was a funny shop. You went in and nobody took any notice of you. They were all in the back sort of gossiping and having a party.'

Fig. 134 (*right*)   Printed silk dress, 1972. Designed by Jean Muir.

Michael Fish opened his Clifford Street shop in 1966, upending the tradition of nearby Savile Row where he had been trained. As neckties buyer from 1962 at Turnbull & Asser, the ties got wider and wider, and Fish claimed that the term 'kipper tie' was a pun on his name.[22] His own shop was described by Nik Cohn as 'a holocaust of see-through voiles, brocades, and spangles, and mini-skirts for men, blinding silks, flower-printed hats' (fig. 133).[23] Later he also designed kaftans for men. In July 1969 it was a Mr Fish white shirt, with huge puffed sleeves, tight bodice to the waist fastened with self-fabric ties, and gathered skirt ballooning to mid-thigh, that Mick Jagger wore to perform at the Rolling Stones' free concert in Hyde Park as he quoted Shelley and released butterflies to the crowd.

In Quant's wake, a new generation of womenswear designers began to emerge, many of them graduates of the fashion course at the Royal College of Art run by the redoubtable Janey Ironside: Marion Foale and Sally Tuffin, David Sassoon, Ossie Clark and Anthony Price. Foale and Tuffin worked out of Carnaby Street. Zandra Rhodes graduated in 1964 with a collection influenced by David Hockney; she went on to produce textiles for Foale & Tuffin before opening the Fulham Road Clothes Shop in 1968 with Sylvia Ayton. Rhodes' artisanal gowns had floating panels of vividly patterned fluid chiffon and silk. Thea Porter worked in an ethnic gypsy style, and Bill Gibb produced knitwear inspired both by medieval and ethnic sources.

Ossie Clark graduated 1964 and moved to Alice Pollock's shop Quorum in 1966. Often using Celia Birtwell's prints, Clark did printed bias-cut dresses, or slithery satin and crêpes, but also masculine tailoring and lean, snakeskin jackets. Quorum, like so many other boutiques, was a social space bringing together pop stars, artists and actors, and Clark made men's shirts in crêpe and satin with frilled fronts. He was one of the few London designers who staged fashion shows, always excessive and remarkable, like Quant before him. His brown print dress from the early seventies (fig. 132) has all the features of his earliest designs and testifies to the enduring success of this style. Similarly, the more austere style of Jean Muir, typified by her meticulously cut dark navy dresses in fine woolen crêpe, is counterbalanced by her unlined printed silk dress (fig. 134). Both garments demonstrate the popularity of print in the early seventies.

COUNTER-CULTURE

In 1966 Jane Ormsby-Gore, an aristocratic early flower child, married Michael Rainey in a secondhand Victorian dress. The press was in thrall to Ormsby-Gore's bohemianism and style (a mixture of retro dresses from the twenties and thirties) as much as to her upper-class origins and house in Westminster. The following year psychedelia descended on London. The *Daily Mirror* reported: 'The kooky kids of '66 have been replaced by the flower girls of '67. Swinging London is awash with Hippie fashions.'[24] As flower power and love-ins took hold, fashionable Londoners responded by turning to secondhand and street markets for their dress. Tuning in and dropping out were hippy deluxe features of west London life in the late 1960s, presaging of what the New York writer Tom Wolfe was to mock in 1974 as 'radical chic'.[25] Yet tuning in and dropping out were also part of a genuinely utopian moment, and 'vintage', as it was only later to be called, offered a real alternative to those Londoners who either did not want, or could not afford, expensive designer clothes. For men, it could signal a hedonistic pleasure in decoration and luxury, as opposed to the rigidity of the tailored suit. They wore velvets, tight military jackets, platform boots, and Indian scarves, beads and bells.[26] The pop artist Peter Blake's 1967 sleeve design for the Beatles' *Sergeant Pepper* album put the four moptops in lurid military uniforms which, like the army surplus clothing that Londoners bought from Lawrence Corner in Euston, mocked militarism and implied a critique of the Vietnam war. By this stage the Beatles no longer went to Dougie Millings for their suits. Having moved to Tommy Nutter, who was revolutionising Savile Row in the second half of the decade, they subsequently gave up suits and took their custom to hippy and psychedelic shops such as I was Lord Kitchener's Valet in the Portobello Road (fig. 135) and even opened their own brief-lived shop, Apple, on Baker Street.

Poised stylistically between Savile Row and Carnaby Street was Blades:

Commercially, [Blades'] greatest strength lay in its ambivalence, the way that it fitted two

Fig. 135   Union Jack printed cotton shirt from I was Lord Kitchener's Valet, 1966–7. Photographed with flared Levis denim jeans, 1971–6. The owner of this shirt later recalled that it was 'hard to remember what one wore . . . At a guess I'd say – flared jeans! The flares would, of course, be triangles of contrasting material sewn into the seam by me.'

Fig. 136 a and b   Herring-bone tweed suit, 1977, by Blades for the interior decorator David Mlinaric. The collar and pocket flaps are edged with velvet.

worlds at once. On the one hand, its clothes were new and riotous; on the other, it had a Georgian frontage in Dover Street, an atmosphere more like a club than a shop and a generous smattering of peerage in its clientele. It was both Pop and Gentleman Amateur at once – pink shirts in the parlour and backgammon in the fitting room.[27]

A double-breasted coat (fig. 137) in the Museum of London's collection was bought off the peg at Blades in 1968. Its big checks, sweeping lapels and generously cut skirts make passing reference to the eighteenth-century squire, but more than anything evoke the swagger of the tall, skinny Chelsea dandies of the 1960s. A green herringbone tweed suit with velvet piping (fig. 136) was bought from Blades nine years later in 1977, just as punk was peaking. It reminds us that the history of London fashion is not linear; the style of the mid-sixties 'peacock revolution' could transform into the new brutalism of punk, but it could equally settle back into the tradition of lovingly cut and tailored gents' suits with a twist, a tradition that has also defined Paul Smith's style for men over three decades.

London's street markets provided a very different source of countercultural fashion from the late 1960s, in particular Portobello Road and Kensington Market. A pair of orange cotton twill sailor trousers (fig. 138) from a boutique was worn with a green Alkasura silk knitted top bought in the early seventies from a market in the King's Road. The creative mixture of vintage, high street and boutique or designer wear is even today considered to be typical of the London look, part of the process of curating the self as both image and object. The twenty-year-old Angela Carter observed of the London of 1967:

Fashion today (real fashion, what real people wear) is a question of style . . . the presentation of the self as a three-dimensional art object, to be wondered at and handled. And this involves a new attitude to the self which is thus adorned. The gaudy rags of the flower children, the element of fancy dress even in 'serious' clothes (the military look, the thirties revival), extravagant and stylised face-painting, wigs, hairpieces, amongst men the extraordi-

Fig. 137   Plaid wool overcoat, 1968. The purchaser of this coat was six foot three inches tall and ten stone in weight when he bought it off the peg from Blades in 1968. He wore it for the following ten years.

Fig. 138   Cotton sailor's bell-bottom trousers, dyed orange, c.1970. Photographed with a synthetic knit shirt by Alkasura. According to the donor, the shirt was 'bought in a market at the time of the hippies . . . and yes, one did wear the bell, the beads and the clumpy shoes'.

Fig. 139 (*left*) *Swingeing London*, 1968. Offset lithograph by Richard Hamilton. A collage of news accounts of the Rolling Stones' 1967 arrest on drugs charges and subsequent trial. The title was a pun on swinging London and the judge's call for a swingeing sentence.

Fig. 140 a and b (*facing*) Printed cotton trouser suit from Biba, c.1973. Worn by Christine Wells, when her husband Keith Wells was a Croydon councillor.

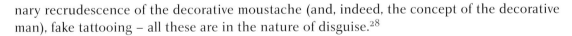

nary recrudescence of the decorative moustache (and, indeed, the concept of the decorative man), fake tattooing – all these are in the nature of disguise.[28]

This element of London style as performance – be it motley, fancy dress or masquerade – is a phenomenon not so readily observed in other fashion capitals. Carter thought that 'this rainbow proliferation of all kinds of fancy dress shows a new freedom many people fear, especially those with something to lose when the frozen, repressive, role-playing world properly starts to melt'.[29] If in subsequent decades role-play came to be rethought as a creative construction of the self, rather than repression, in either case the result is the same: extreme dressing up. Carter understood the symbolic value of clothing when she described the 1967 drugs trial of Mick Jagger and the art dealer Robert Fraser as 'an elegant confrontation of sartorial symbolism in generation warfare: the judge in ritually potent robes and wig, invoking the doom of his age and class on the beautiful children in frills and sunset colours' (fig. 139).[30] Towards the end of the 1960s, the increasingly decadent, drug-fuelled aesthetic was reflected in fashion photography and in film.

The evanescent images of Antonioni's *Blow-Up* (1966) and the fluid, disintegrating personae of Nick Roeg and Donald Cammell's *Performance* (1968, released 1972) capture the growing instability of the time.

In 1973 Biba moved for the third time, from its Kensington High Street boutique to a vast retro emporium in the revamped department store Derry & Toms on Kensington High Street. A Biba trouser suit from 1973, with its retro 1930s-style flower print, typifies the silhouette of the time: narrow upper arms, padded shoulders, lean-cut torso and tight hipster trousers that flared from the hips, with heavy turn-ups that added to the weight and were worn with platform shoes to increase the length of the leg (fig. 140). In its final home, the enormously expanded Biba sold everything from specially packaged baked beans to dark, chocolate-coloured satin sheets. A total shopping experience, the opulent décor drew on art nouveau and 1930s influences; it was decadent, romantic and nostalgic, featuring black glass counters and parlour palms. Hulanicki's determination to pursue her vision set her at odds with her backers and the shop closed in 1975. A fundamental desire to create a new kind of shop, combined with total lack of respect for conventional retailing and business wisdom, and a refusal to water down their designs for the mass-market, characterised many of the sixties designer retailers. Bedevilled by the tension between creativity and commerce, London fashion shone brightly in the sixties, but could not sustain itself and burnt out faster than less innovative enterprises.

By the early 1970s the boutique boom of the sixties was largely over. Few had ever been run conventionally and many closed due to excessive shoplifting, high running costs, or the owners' fundamental lack of interest in the business side. South Molton Street and the West End were fashionable areas, but the stock was more international, selling French and Italian brands. One exception was Tommy Roberts who opened his Mr Freedom boutique, first on the old King's Road site of Hung on You, then in Kensington Church Street. Against the grain of contemporary boutiques that still dealt in hippy dress and nostalgia, Roberts promoted brash, pop art fashion with giant platform boots and long T-shirt dresses appliquéd with satin stars, thunderbolts and ice-cream cones. Although short-lived, the boutique was immediately successful and its fusion of fifties retro, cartoon imagery and kitsch was widely copied as pop art fashion by Parisian couturiers as well as by pirates. Art and fashion also crossed over in the London design and manufacturing company Ritva in 1971. The Ritva Man's limited-edition sweaters had motifs designed by London artists David Hockney, Allen Jones, Elisabeth Frink and Patrick Hughes. Specially designed perspex display boxes could be ordered in which to display the sweaters when they were not being worn (fig. 141).

While the decadent hippy look persisted well into the 1970s and, indeed, was one of the principal styles that punk revolted against in 1976, the early seventies also saw the arrival of glam rock. A number of fashion designers made clothes for musicians, such as Zandra Rhodes' designs for Freddy Mercury of Queen, and the Michael Fish dress David Bowie wore on the sleeve of *The Man Who Sold the World*. As Ziggy Stardust, Bowie was dressed by Freddie Burretti in stacked boots and jump suits, his hair feather-cut and streaked green or orange, his eyelids slicked or glittered. Bryan Ferry and Roxy Music were dressed with camp Hollywood glamour by Anthony Price, another Royal College of Art graduate. By contrast, Ian Dury, then lead singer with Kilburn and the High Roads, the antithesis of glam rock, claimed an indigenous London advantage for his stage clothes that mixed jumble-sale clobber and East End flash:

> We looked unique, dressed unique. We were all art school babies who knew what we were doing. We were sharper than Bryan Ferry because we come from London, not Newcastle, with due respect: sharp, man, on the case. We weren't designer, because we bought secondhand. But back then, secondhand was wide open.[31]

Fig. 141 a and b   The Ritva Man sweater, 1971. Acrylic sweater with a central motif designed by the artist Allen Jones for The Ritva Man. The colours and overall design were chosen by the designer Mike Ross who was co-founder and owner of the Ritva labels with his wife, Ritva Ross.

In the reception Siouxsie removed her mac, revealing a simple black dress with a plunging V neckline, black net loosely covering her pert breasts. A home-made swastika flash was safety-pinned to a red armband. Black strap stilettos, studs gleaming, bound her feet; fishnet tights and black vinyl stockings her legs. Her short black hair was flecked with red flames.[1]

Siouxsie Sioux was having a drink at the lesbian bar Louise's in Soho's Poland Street, one of the few places that let punks in. It was October 1976, and Siouxsie and the Banshees had just débuted at the 100 Club on Oxford Street, where she famously crossed the divide between audience and stage by simply getting up and performing. Both on and off stage, Siouxsie wore the mixed uniforms of sexual fetishism, poor taste and moral outrage that characterised the brief moment of punk music from 1976 to early 1977.[2] Like other punk performers, many of her clothes came from Malcolm McLaren and Vivienne Westwood's shop Sex at 430 King's Road, the previous site of Hung On You. Its fascia was obscured by the shop sign, the letters S–E–X spelt out in four-foot-high pink rubber capitals; inside it sold fetish and bondage outfits and, later, clothes with anarchist or Situationist slogans. Before it became Sex in 1974, the shop had sold Ted and biker styles under the name Let It Rock (1971) and then Too Fast to Live, Too Young to Die (1973).

With hindsight, McLaren felt that 'fashion seemed to be the place where music and art came together'.[3] Asked at the time if clothes were all that important, Joe Strummer, lead singer of the Clash, replied laconically 'like trousers, like brain'.[4] Contemptuous of flares and all who wore them, punks wore rubber or fishnet stockings; torn and stained T-shirts; tight drainpipe jeans or baggy black combats with cuffed hems; and ragged cropped hair in peroxide blonde or day-glo colours. Sex sold mohair jumpers with holes, jeans with vinyl panels and zips inserted between the legs or at the back of the thighs, and its notorious T-shirts. Maxims from Rousseau and slogans from the Situationists had decorated the premises since 1974; in 1975 the range of approximately twenty T-shirts extended the provocation with explicit references to paedophilia, pornography and violence against women.[5]

One of these sleeveless T-shirts, now belonging to the Museum of London, bears a text from the Scottish writer Alexander Trocchi's pornographic book of lesbian fantasies *School for Wives* (fig. 143). Others included the Cambridge rapist T-shirt and Tom of Finland's two cowboys naked from the waist down, their flaccid penises not quite touching. In 1976, Sex was closed for remodelling; it reopened in September as Seditionaries. It sold 'Anarchy' and 'Destroy' T-shirts, parachute shirts with rip cords, and bondage trousers. Peter York called it 'a shop for the elite of Radical Displacement'.[6] In 1977, the year of the Queen's jubilee,

Fig. 142   Satvinder, 1990. Photographed by Corinne Day for *The Face.* Courtesty of Corinne Day. (Copyright Corinne Day 1990).

Fig. 143   Sex T-shirt, 1975. White cotton printed with text from Alexander Trocchi's *School for Wives* with slit opening above the bust. Designed by Vivienne Westwood and Malcolm McLaren. The T-shirt was stitched together with the raw edges on the outside.

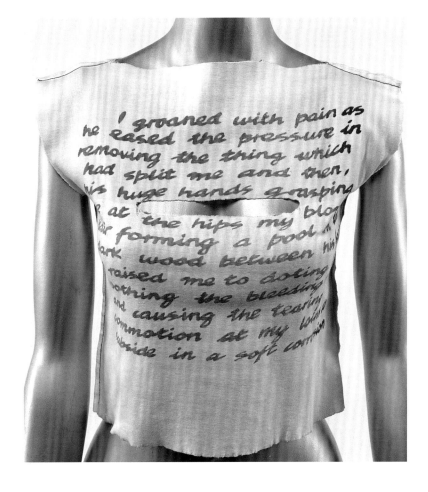

Fig. 144   The Sex Pistols' single, 'God Save the Queen', 1977. The Virgin record sleeve, based on Cecil Beaton's official portrait of the queen, was designed by Jamie Reid as an anti-Jubilee protest. Reid's graphics were intended to subvert the status quo through its own means. He designed a whole range of images on this theme, including a famous one of the queen with a safety pin through her nose, for the record's promotional campaign.

Jamie Reid's graphics for the Sex Pistols' single 'God Save the Queen' (fig. 144) were adapted for T-shirts and backdrops showing the Queen with a safety pin through her nose.

In the basement of number 153, at the other end of the King's Road, was Acme Attractions. The shop's clientele and merchandise were more hybrid than Sex's. Punks might invoke 'white dread' but, as imagined by Westwood and McLaren, their cultural references derived from a European history of dissent. Acme drew instead on a multicultural vibe from across London and its suburbs, attracting soul boys from out of town, south London wide-boys as well as punks and ex-Mods, many of whom went on to become New Romantics in the early eighties. Its manager Don Letts, who was to form Big Audio Dynamite with Mick Jones of the Clash in the 1980s, had dreads to his waist and played dub reggae from the basement shop. The clothes were from the forties, fifties and sixties, drawing on a variety of sharp youth styles from earlier decades. Typical Acme looks included vintage short-sleeved shirts, plastic sandals and bright mohair jumpers. Yet it did not exclude punk, and Don Letts wore the bondage trousers that, for Westwood, implied 'commitment', even if it was not clear to what or to whom. Letts had to defend his bondage trousers – and punk itself – against Bob Marley's criticisms (punks were his friends, said Letts, and besides, the trousers contained plenty of hiding places for weed). The result, as Paul Gorman has observed, was Marley's single 'Punky Reggae Party' that name-checks the principal punk exponents. The

anecdote demonstrates the way a small creative retail space can facilitate the cross-pollination of both musical styles and subcultural affiliations.[7]

Like the boutiques of the sixties, Acme and Sex were first and foremost social rather than retail spaces. They marked another moment when fashion and pop came together in the history of London. Over the following decade, Acme underwent many transformations as it became Boy and went mainstream. Quite unlike most cutting-edge small London retailers, by 1988 Boy had franchises from Los Angeles to Tokyo. Its lycra and clubwear and the famous 'Boy' baseball caps were worn worldwide by personalities from Andy Warhol to Princess Diana. The style and ethos, however, had changed completely in the process.

DIY AESTHETICS

By late 1977, punk music had peaked. The mohican haircut (fig. 145) that developed afterwards (and was so frequently reproduced on London postcards for tourists) was never a part of the original look. Although punk had been a relatively small phenomenon in a few British cities, principally London, Manchester and Liverpool, it catalysed both mainstream fashion and subcultural style well into the early 1980s. In the fashion industry, there were no more flares and hippy beads; trousers were narrow or peg-topped. Subculturally, a plethora of styles flourished, from rockabilly

Fig. 145   Latter-day punks with Mohican hair at a festival in Hyde Park, 1982. Photograph by Henry Grant. (Henry Grant Collection, Museum of London).

Fig. 146   Denim jacket, c.1982.
Customised with a crucifix image and
Oi slogans.

Fig. 147   Mohair hand-knitted punk
sweater, c.1980.

to two-tone to neo-Ted, all documented by the new independent magazines *The Face, i-D* and
Blitz. A young woman's denim jacket from the early eighties (fig. 146) is customised with the slogans 'Strength through Oi!' and 'Skins of the 80s'. Oi was speed punk music with extreme right-
wing affiliations, led by the notorious skinhead group Screwdriver. The Do-It-Yourself ethic of
this jacket, as well as its flirtation with taboo symbols such as the crucifix, testify to punk's influence, despite the very different political agenda. At the same time, more benign multicultural
influences – two-tone, rudies, ska – worked on pop fashion through bands such as the Specials.[8]

It was above all the DIY aesthetic inherited from punk that characterised the following decade.
Innovative fashion from groundbreaking labels did not come cheap, but the aesthetic was free for
all to customise. A hand-knitted mohair sweater in the collection of the Museum of London (fig.
147) is clearly in the style of the Sex and Acme mohair jumpers of the mid-seventies. The stylist
Judy Blame recalled:

We couldn't really afford the Seditionaries clothes or whatever, so we would do the jumble sale, buy a suit, throw a bucket of paint over it, cut it up, join it back together with safety pins – it was much more homemade. It was better for me. I think that's where I get that attitude where you can use anything, it's not a money thing, it's a visual, statement thing. I didn't really know where to put my creative energy, so I put it on myself, basically – dressing up, dyeing my hair, making clothes. But I didn't see it as a job or anything. I just saw it as ... going to college without going to college. Education. Educating yourself.[9]

Blame (his name was as fabricated as his look) was at the forefront of the 1980s charity-shop stylists whose magpie aesthetic – 'from mad drag to alien'– recycled cultural detritus as cutting-edge imagery for independent magazines such as *i-D* in the post-punk period.[10] The first issues of *i-D,* produced by ex-*Vogue* art director Terry Jones, were xeroxed pages loosely stapled together behind a coloured cover. Its 'straight-up' pages reproduced the street as a catwalk identity parade on pages that showed 'ordinary' people (fig. 148). Based on the mugshot and tabloid pictures of punks, the 'straight-up' idea derived from the earlier *Nova* and reportage on punk dress, such as Terry Jones' *Not Another Punk Book!* (1978).[11]

Around 1980 Bowie-inspired cross-dressing and extreme make-up turned a new 'cult with no name' into 'Blitz kids' (after the Covent Garden club they frequented) or New Romantics. They wore an eclectic mixture of theatrical costumes and creatively remade secondhand clothing. Their white ruffled shirts came from PX in Covent Garden. In a backlash against punk, anyone in Seditionaries clothes was turned away from the Blitz club. The high-maintenance look changed daily and was predicated on the idea of the self as a work of art, something to be continually rescripted in the club culture of the early eighties by figures such as Boy George, the designer Stephen Linard, and club hosts Philip Sallon and Steve Strange. Spandau Ballet exported the look on their 1981 New York tour. That year Boy George worked with the designer Sue Clowes to develop his Culture Club look and together they opened their shop, the Foundry. Like Westwood, Clowes looked to history and culture for her references. The early eighties inaugurated a histori-cising tendency that would also typify London fashion during the nineties. Clowes' imagery fused punk with Judaism and Catholicism, and George put the look together with dreads, rasta hats and full make-up.

The tendency to make a creative hybrid out of the past, pillaging history like an image bank to be raided, was later to characterise the designs of John Galliano well into the 1990s. Just as DJs mixed old music into something new, so designers mixed cultures and histories to produce a London look. Something of this London eclecticism comes across in Wendy Dagworthy's multi-

Fig. 148 *i-D,* No. 6, 1981. The magazine's 'straight-up' pages mimicked the DIY aesthetic of punk fanzines, turning the street into a catwalk with their vox pop coverage of real people collaged together from different contexts. In this spread 'Paul', in the centre of the group, is wearing a Westwood Pirates shirt; 'two blokes' on the right typify an emerging gay style at London's Heaven club and, on the left, 'Denis and M' exemplify the early eighties recycling of sharp black urban musical styles from previous decades. Photographs by Susana Frye and James Palmer. Courtesy of *i-D* magazine.

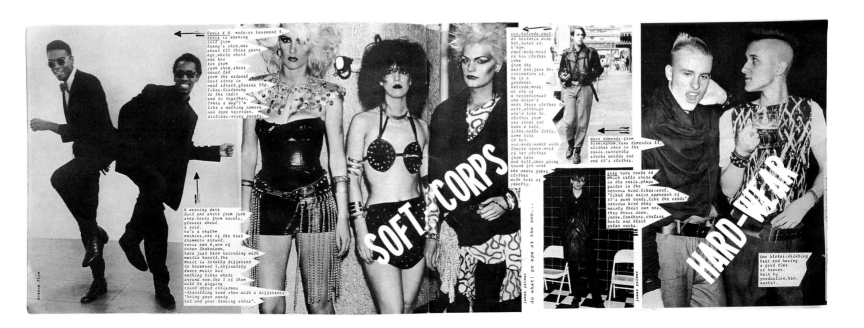

Fig. 149   Hand-woven cotton outfit, spring/summer 1982. Designer Wendy Dagworthy based the shape of the trousers on those worn by Thai fishermen. She stated that her 'design signature was her ability to recontextualise her inspirational sources . . . drawn from traditional fabrics and ethnic cultures and then transposed into contemporary designs'.

Fig. 150 a and b   Vivienne Westwood wool jacket, autumn/winter 1983. Printed with drawings by graffiti Keith Haring (1958–90). The Witches collection was the final collaboration between Westwood & McLaren.

layered Ikat outfit with its cultural mix of non-European garment types (fig. 149). Its silhouette – balanced and surprisingly unbulky given how many layers there are – is similar to Westwood's Buffalo collection, with its padded satin bras and skirts layered upon skirts, accessorised with big Peruvian hats.

Westwood split from McLaren in 1983. The period up to 1984 was one of her most creative and assured. From World's End, as her shop was now called, she produced her Pirate, Savage, Buffalo, Hobo-Punkature and Witches collections. The Witches collection of 1983 mixed street and sportswear, tubular cotton skirts, clumpy trainers, fluorescent colours and graphics by the American artist Keith Haring. Westwood's eccentric approach to cutting was based on the willful misinterpretation of historical dress that she had first explored in the Pirate collection. The cut of the jacket (fig. 150) is square, the waist gathered from the side of the square to the middle, the sleeve cut square and gusseted to a point at elbow and shoulder. Westwood maintained that for all its bagginess, the jacket is articulated in relation to the body.[12]

Amalgamating body and clothing through unorthodox cutting was also a feature of David Holah and Stevie Stewart's label BodyMap. Their first collection for spring/summer 1984, *Querelle Meets Olive Oyle*, used soft cotton jersey with Hilde Smith's black and white prints. Their second

collection featured asymmetrical portholes cut into the torso of their fitted cotton dresses and boxer shorts over bold, hooped tights with cropped wrap tops, all in graphic red, white and black (fig. 151). BodyMap developed a different sense of the body to the Japanese-inspired trend towards baggy, black, androgynous clothing that was fashionable at the time. Their shows were innovative too; models were replaced with family members, including mums, as well as performers, pop stars, dancers and singers. At Crolla, by contrast, Scott Crolla and Georgina Godley mixed ikats, chintz, velvets and brocades. Godley later produced knitted silk dresses with wired seams and unorthodox padding that mimicked muscles or pregnancy.

Punk's sloganeering lingered in the anti-establishment clothes of Katherine Hamnett. Her 1984 crumpled combats in parachute silk and cotton, and a range of 'Save the World' T-shirts with political slogans such as 'WORLDWIDE NUCLEAR BAN NOW' were sparked by European anxieties about the siting of American nuclear missiles on European airbases such as Greenham Common. Hamnett made the silk 'US GO HOME' version for the retailer Joseph who declined to stock them on the basis that many of his customers were American (fig. 152 b). With the publicist Lynne Franks and her colleague Heather Lambert, Hamnett then drove to Greenham Common and offered the T-shirts to members of the women's peace camp who also declined to wear them,

several of them also being Americans. Hamnett herself famously wore her '58% DON'T WANT PERSHING' T-shirt to meet prime minister Margaret Thatcher at Downing Street. The band Frankie goes to Hollywood plagiarised her slogan T-shirts to publicise their single 'Relax'. They appeared on stage in T-shirts that read 'FRANKIE SAYS RELAX' and the look was further debased in Wham!'s 'Wake Me Up Before You Go-Go' video. The bands satirically undercut Hamnett's earnestness, using the T-shirts' very urban posturing to refuse to take the world too seriously.

THE BUZZ OF BUSINESSS

Many of London's most innovative designers from Mary Quant to Paul Smith started their careers by opening shops selling interesting clothes, often a mix of their own and those of other designers. The history of London fashion has a direct connection to its city zones and the experience of shopping. Creating individual and interesting retail spaces has always been part of this. In the early eighties, a collective of designers including Willy Brown opened Demob in a former fishmonger's shop in Beak Street, Soho. While the shop fittings evoked the forties and fifties, with a hair salon and soda fountain added, the clothes plundered a range of twentieth-century styles from the First World War to Utility for women, and rockabilly for men.

Mid-eighties London fashion had a vibrant buzz. In business terms it was a good time for independent companies such as Betty Jackson, Bernstock & Spiers, John Flett, Richmond Cornejo,

Fig. 152 a, b (*above*)   Katherine Hamnett T-shirts, *c.*1984.

Fig. 151 (*facing*)   BodyMap, The Cat in the Hat Takes a Rumble with the Techno Fish collection, autumn/winter 1984. BodyMap consisted of fashion designers, David Holah and Stevie Stewart, and the textile designer Hilde Smith who worked with them to produce these bold, graphic prints on sweat-shirting and cotton jersey. Photograph by Niall McInerney.

Fig. 153 Paul Smith jacket, autumn/winter 2002. Velvet, decorated with a hand-painted flower.

Wendy Dagworthy, Jasper Conran, Christopher Nemeth & Paul Howie, who was married to Lynne Franks (the PR guru later satirised as Edina in the television series *Absolutely Fabulous*). Later in the decade, Hyper Hyper in Kensington High Street provided an important forum for a range of independent London designers. Christopher New, who opened his first menswear shop in Dean Street in 1984, recalls that it was easy to make money then; the economy was booming, West End rents were low, the yen was strong and many Japanese buyers sought out individualistic London fashion.

In 1984 the BodyMap designer Stevie Stewart wrote: 'There is a new generation emerging throughout England today, particularly from London which is now looked upon by the rest of the world as a focal point of creative energy in fashion, film, video, music and dance'.[13] She identified a number of features that typified London fashion as she saw it: a vibrant small independent press that reported on new talent and was read world-wide; the importance of social life, clubs and music to generate innovative fashion ('humour is combined with hard work'); the traditional association of the city with youth and subculture; the interaction of fashion and music, citing Boy George and Helen Terry of Culture Club, and Haysi Fantayzee whose Jeremy Healy was later to DJ for John Galliano's shows in Paris as well as London; and finally the way that financial necessity required individuals to work in more than one field, such as fashion *and* club promotion, DJ-ing, filmmaking, selling accessories and modelling.[14] She commented on the fertile crossovers between BodyMap and filmmaker John Maybury, dancer Michael Clark and Leigh Bowery, then an aspiring fashion designer.

A key figure of the eighties scene in London, Bowery's true vocation was endlessly to recreate himself as a glamorous object. The London art dealer Anthony D'Offay understood this when, in 1988, he installed Bowery as a living performance in his Dering Street gallery window every day for a week. Among his hundreds of looks, one from 1984 has him sporting 'blue face and body make-up, enormous rubberised platform shoes, oversize shirts with four or six sleeves and leatherette caps decorated with diamanté, sequins, pearls and stars'.[15] This theatricalisation of the self extended to Bowery's friend and flatmate Trojan who cut his ear (in a parody of Van Gogh) 'out of boredom'. At Taboo, the club Bowery hosted from 1985, the rule was 'dress as though your life depends on it, or don't bother'.[16]

From the mid-eighties Vivienne Westwood's designs made fewer overt challenges to the *status quo*. Instead she began to rework historical dress in a modern idiom, as if to take its symbolic power and make it her own. Her 1986 mini-crini combined the Victorian crinoline with the sixties mini. She paired it with a fake ermine cape and tweed jacket to refer to the current queen. Ten years later she styled herself for a photograph as Queen Elizabeth I. The mini-crini's silhouette was widely copied in the eighties (in Christian Lacroix's puffball skirt, for instance), but the eccentricity of the original was lost in translation. From the late eighties and into the 1990s, Westwood's grandiose designs constructed an imaginary aristocratic past, with swaggering tartans, bunched taffeta, tailored tweeds and painted stays.[17] In the 1980s she became, like Quant before her, a very successful export, as much for her ideas as her clothes. She had an Italian backer, moved her manufacturing to Italy, was successful in international markets, and was invited to show in Japan and France in 1983. She helped to define Britishness overseas and was courted by politicians.[18]

In the mid-eighties, while Japanese designers were catering to the upper end of the menswear market, a gap in the middle was filled by Demob and designers associated with the club scene. The market was created partly by the changing image of men in *i-D* and *The Face*, which fostered a new consumer desire, no longer targeted at gay men alone.[19] In the early eighties, *i-D, The Face* and *Blitz* had documented fashionable male androgyny and camp extravagance in the club scene. Although their circulation was relatively low, these magazines were disproportionately influential because they were read by so many important taste-makers in the industry, both at home and abroad. In late 1986 Nick Logan, publisher of *The Face*, launched *Arena,* an equivalent title dedicated exclusively to men's fashion. New designers included the Duffer of St George, selling initially from Camden Market, Red or Dead and Pam Hogg. By the late eighties Duffer catered to a knowing male market that was interested in streetwear and the emerging acid house scene at the Shoom! club but, equally, not averse to a label or a nicely designed detail.

Before then, Paul Smith was the most influential figure in the design and retail of menswear. Smith moved from Nottingham to London and opened his first shop in Floral Street in 1979. Expanding his company in the 1980s, he was one of the few London-based designers with a local identity who also sold on an international scale, capitalising equally on his design and business skills. His retail outfits as far afield as Tokyo lovingly recreated the look of a traditional English gents' outfitter. The idea of Smith as a shopkeeper, always retaining his Floral Street base, was crucial. The business traded not on a corporate identity but on the idea of England as a nation of shopkeepers. Many fashionable figures have traded on either this stereotype, or on another, the idea of the eccentric embraced, for example, by Vivienne Westwood.

In the eighties the Paul Smith look became associated with the stereotype of the 'yuppie', whose much-mocked filofaxes sold alongside other quirky accessories in his shops. But the style outlived the stereotype into the next decade. Over nearly thirty years, he has continued to sell a range of formal and casual menswear that relies on traditional details, fabric or cut but always incorporates a hidden quirk or twist – a subtly narrowed lapel, a floral lining to a denim shirt

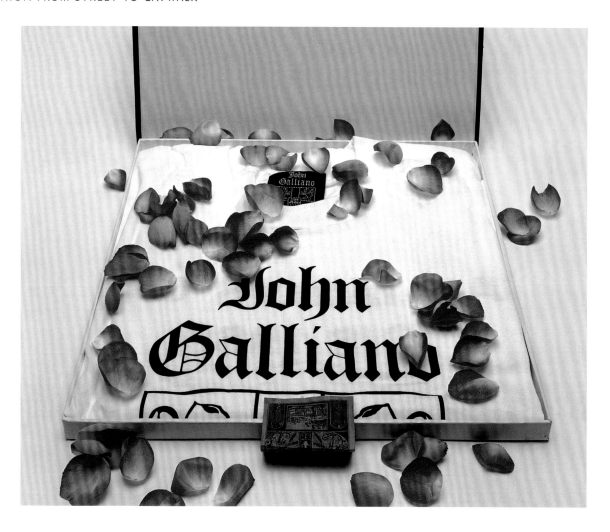

Fig. 154 John Galliano invitation/pro-motional gift, 1989. This boxed T-shirt was given to members of the press invited to Galliano's spring/summer 1989 collection. The box also contained rose petals and six postcards detailing the designer's work.

cuff, or a hand-painted flower on a velvet suit (fig. 153). In the nineties such innovation continued to flow from a new generation of tailors including Timothy Everest, Richard James and Ozwald Boateng whose work embraced the Savile Row tradition of tailoring while simultaneously issuing a witty challenge to it as it engaged with other, international registers of style.

At the other end of the scale to Paul Smith, the combination of high visibility and financial impecuniousness more typical of London fashion designers was exemplified by John Galliano. His 1984 graduation collection, Les Incroyables, based on post-revolutionary France, was bought by the London fashion shop Browns where it filled the entire window display. Galliano continued to design in his own name during the late 1980s and early 1990s, working closely with his influential 'muse' and assistant, Lady Amanda Harlech, on a series of collections that fused history, cinema and popular culture in dramatically styled shows.[20] In 1988 he won the Designer of the Year award for his Blanche Dubois collection. His shows, even when produced on a shoestring budget, were always spectacular productions with meticulous attention to detail, such as the promotional gift for the spring/summer 1989 season, a T-shirt in a rose-petal-strewn box (fig. 154).

Despite gaining a cult following and the respect of the industry, Galliano's business was precarious. After several backers came and went, he moved to Paris in 1989, and in 1993 the influential editor of New York *Vogue,* Anna Wintour, came to his aid. He staged a landmark show in a private house in Paris whose rooms he dressed like a film set, with overturned chairs and unmade beds scattered with rose petals. In July 1995 he was appointed principal designer at Givenchy where he remained for three seasons before moving to Dior, producing his first haute couture collection in January 1997. With the backing of a major Parisian couture house, Galliano was able to do justice to the breadth of his vision, using his earnings from Dior to fund his John Galliano

label. Galliano's shows recreated a snowy rooftop, a circus ring or an enchanted forest; always he transformed the space to impose his fantasy on it. His invitations came in the form of a rusty key, a ballet slipper, a charm bracelet inside a Russian doll, or a schoolgirl's report.

Alongside Alexander McQueen, Galliano was largely responsible for the spectacular and outrageous shows that characterised the late 1990s. As Stéphane Wagner of the Institut Français de la Mode said in 1997: 'If we accept that much of haute couture is about squeezing out maximum media coverage – good or bad – then the more spectacular the presentation and collection, the better. And from that point the English are the best by far.'[21] In the late 1990s, the more conservative Parisian couture houses hired three British designers to revive their flagging fortunes: Galliano at Dior, Alexander McQueen who succeeded him at Givenchy, and Stella McCartney at Chloé.

During the eighties high fashion had tended to dominate, although retail innovation came from Browns in South Molton Street, and Jones in Covent Garden and the King's Road. However both shops specialised in international rather than specifically London design. Following the boom years of the mid-eighties in London, the recession of the early nineties caused a number of design companies to go to the wall, and the mood of London fashion was lacklustre, only enlivened by Rifat Ozbek's all-white New Age collection in 1990 and his subsequent rainbow-coloured sequined one. Originally from Turkey, Ozbek made London his home, but his hybrid collections might look to Indonesia, central Europe or north Africa for their influences.

The new wave of innovative and experimental fashion from the mid-nineties that peaked towards the turn of the century put London back on the map internationally (even if not all its participants were equally commercial).[22] It did so not only through idiosyncratic design, but equally through a range of dramatic fashion shows intended for maximum press impact rather

Fig. 155 Finale of Alexander McQueen's autumn/winter 1998 show. Drawing on the story of Joan of Arc, the catwalk simulated black lava and the show culminated with a ring of fire that sprang up on the catwalk trapping the model in the centre. Photograph by Niall McInerney. (Courtesy of Alexander McQueen. Copyright Niall McInerney).

than production. Such images emanated from London but were broadcast round the world (fig. 157). Fabio Piras described this as 'a certain synergy' that came out of the recession, and designated his generation of Central Saint Martins graduates, spearheaded by Alexander McQueen who graduated in 1992, 'fashion desperadoes'.[23] Compared to Paris or Milan, there was relatively little infrastructure in London fashion and graduates wishing to establish themselves or attract a backer required the press coverage guaranteed by staging polemical, sometimes shocking, fashion spectacles.

Darkly romantic, with a harsh vision of history and politics, McQueen's designs differed from the more straightforwardly romantic output of Galliano or Westwood. His inspirations were as likely to be cult films by Kubrick, Pasolini or Hitchcock, or seventeenth-century anatomical plates, as previous fashion designers. His early designs included the low-slung and cleavage-revealing 'bumster' trousers; he maintained a fascination with highly structured corsets and sharp tailoring, as well as with historical cut and detailing. However the victimised look of his early models gave way in the late 1990s to an Amazonian version of female glamour as a form of terror. McQueen introduced extraordinary narrative and aesthetic content to his runway shows.

Fig. 157 (*above*)   Hussein Chalayan, After Words, autumn/winter 2000, a show based on the themes of exile and migrancy. The chair covers convert into dresses, the chairs into suitcases and the table into a tiered wooden skirt. Photograph by Chris Moore. (Courtesy of Hussein Chalayan. Copyright Chris Moore).

Fig. 156 (*facing*)   Alexander McQueen silk chiffon dress, autumn/winter 2003. Decorated with metallic embroidery.

Fig. 158 Sophia Kokosalaki dress, autumn/winter 2002. Black jersey with lattice-work shoulder-piece.

Fig. 159 Eley Kishimoto coat, spring/summer 2003. Hand-printed cotton.

Styling, showmanship and dramatic presentation became as important as the design of the clothes; models walked on water, were drenched in 'golden showers' on an ink-flooded catwalk, or surrounded by rings of flame (fig. 155). The early shows were put together on minimal budgets, assisted by models, make-up artists, stylists and producers prepared to work for nothing. His creative director Katy England played an important role in both the development of his aesthetic and the design and styling of his shows. He commissioned accessories for his shows from Dai Rees and jewellers Shaun Lean and Naomi Filmer and worked with innovative film, video and pop producers.

In October 1996, aged twenty-seven, McQueen was appointed designer-in-chief at Givenchy in Paris, replacing Galliano who went to Christian Dior. Although his style was toned down at Givenchy, it retained its essential features until his departure in 2001. In December 2000 McQueen sold a controlling share in his business to Gucci. The sale signalled an attempt to transform a small-scale London label into a global luxury brand. Having already stopped showing in London in favour of Paris, he went on to launch a perfume and open flagship stores interna-

tionally, selling the more restrained styles of his subsequent work (fig. 156). In 2003 he was awarded a CBE for his services to the fashion industry.

In 1993 the third of the most distinctively innovative London designers of the nineties, Hussein Chalayan, graduated from Central Saint Martins with a collection that used rusted fabric that had been buried in a friend's garden for six weeks. Unlike Galliano and McQueen, Chalayan worked largely independently of the big fashion conglomerates, apart from a period of designing for Tse in New York. His spectacular London shows throughout the 1990s resembled art installations in modernist spaces, often using avant-garde musicians. His designs referred to themes unusual for a fashion designer: architecture, science, technology, travel and exile (fig. 157). He printed dresses with the flight paths of aeroplanes, or suspended them on the catwalk from helium-filled balloons. He used unusual fabric such as the paper-like Tyvek for an 'airmail' dress that could be folded up and sent in the post; hard resin for showpieces such as the remote controlled dresses; and an electrically wired hem with a 'memory' that lifted the skirts of a red dress on the catwalk so that it retained its new shape afterwards.

Fig. 160 Fake London miniskirt and vest, 2002. Denim miniskirt with attached elastic suspender and khaki green shell top with side lacing.

BREWING FUSION

In the late nineties, Chalayan, too, stopped showing in London and began to show in Paris. With the departure of the three most spectacular showmen of London fashion to Paris by the late nineties, many felt that London Fashion Week had lost its edge. But it is in the nature of the British fashion industry, which is tiny compared to others, that at a certain stage in a designer's progress they must move onward to more global markets, freeing up space for new-comers to the industry. Other British designers such as Luella Bartley and Matthew Williamson have moved their shows to New York. Meanwhile the British system of fashion education continued to produce new, young, interesting designers, such as Sophia Kokosalaki (fig. 158) and Eley Kishimoto (fig. 159). For better or worse, it is largely for this freshness that overseas fashion buyers look to London.

Fig. 162 (*above*)   Fashion photograph by Jason Evans (Travis), *i-D*, July 1991. Styling by Simon Foxton, model Edward Enninful, suit by Swaine & Adeney. Courtesy of Jason Evans. (Copyright Jason Evans 1991).

Fig. 160 (*facing*)   Vexed Generation parka, trousers and backpack, 1996. Made from nylon 66 (neobalistic nylon).

The late nineties were, like the mid-sixties, a productive period for the 'creative industries' in London.[24] Journalists commented on the rise of Brit-pop (bands like Oasis, Blur and Suede) and on Brit-art (the YBAs, young British artists such as Damien Hirst and Sarah Lucas).[25] Stella McCartney's slip dresses were promoted as the signature of the 'London girl', an insouciant Notting Hill Gate style that reprised the themes of Carnaby Street and the dollybird that had marked 'swinging London' in the 1960s. International models originating from London included Kate Moss and Naomi Campbell. The cover of the British edition of *Vanity Fair* in February 1997 epitomised the theme of Cool Britannia and new London-based magazines included *Don't Tell It*, *SleazeNation* and *Dazed & Confused*. The decade remained an influential one for new photography, fashion photography in particular. The work of Juergen Teller, Corinne Day, David Sims and Nick Knight defined the look of the mid-decade. Later photographers included Elaine Constantine and Norbert Schoerner.

Alongside McQueen, Galliano, Chalayan and a host of other designers came another wave of innovative small shops in the London tradition, such as the Hoxton Boutique, Koh Samui and Pineal Eye. In tandem, a number of highly diverse, small design companies flourished throughout the 1990s. Antoni and Alison, known for their original slogan T-shirts sold in vacuum-packaging, opened a quirky shop called Factory of Light on Rosebery Avenue. From 1995 Fake London, designed by the Spanish Desiré Mejer, cut up and recycled cashmere, making iconoclastic jumpers that subverted the symbols of nationhood, such as the Union Jack in Rasta colours, to reflect the hybridity of the real London. Its logo and label on a denim skirt and khaki vest top (fig. 160) announce them to be 'Fake London Genius'. From the beginning of the decade, the designers Joe Hunter and Adam Thorpe worked as Vexed Generation to produce socially aware agitprop fashion that reflected both designers' experience of life on the London streets: surveillance (a hood that conceals the face), the environment (a sleeve pocket for an anti-pollution mask), the quick change (a skirt that zips into a pair of trousers) (fig. 160).

The diversity of London cultural identities at the beginning of the 1990s can be glimpsed in two photographs from the start of the decade. Corinne Day's photograph in *The Face* shows Satvinder, a young Sikh in a Union Jack T-shirt (fig. 141). For *i-D* Travis (Jason Evans) photographed the black model and fashion editor Edward Enninful in a riding jacket and plus twos, a monocle round his neck (fig. 161). The parody of upper-class country gentleman is cemented by the backdrop of suburban London pebbledash and mock-Tudor door.[26] During the second half of the twentieth century, the cultural diversity of London has fed into its fashion culture in many ways, not least through music and subculture. In the early 1990s, Soul II Soul was a London-based label, not just a band. Like So Solid Crew in the mid- to late 1990s, it was also a collective. So Solid Crew was a typical London hybrid, fusing garage, jungle and rap with a south London accent. The look mixed designer fashion with lovers' rock, as when furry Kangol hats were worn back to front in a south London wide-boy look. In the same period, Bangra represented the coming of age of Asian and Indian youth in British culture. Most black and Asian music-based subcultures in London were hybrids of movements that began outside Britain: Rastafarianism (the Caribbean), Hip-hop (the USA) and Ragga (Jamaica). They were then 'customised' locally: the tight clothes and brash jewellery of Ragga, for example, journeyed from Kingston, Jamaica, via Dalston, London, to their London incarnation. Meanwhile shops such as Zee Clothing on Islington's Upper Street and in the Roman Road in the East End typified the way an independent retailer might sell a style and a way of wearing clothes to a clientele of black Londoners by stocking an edited and fine-tuned range of menswear, from Paul Smith to Gucci.[27]

While fashion manufacturing in Britain continued to decline in the 1990s, various attempts were made to use the cultural capital of London 'names', principally through chain store endorsement of designers such as Hussein Chalayan at Top Shop and Jasper Conran at Debenham's. Using its flagship store in London's Oxford Circus as a laboratory for the rest of the chain, Top Shop's just-in-time production methods enabled it to try out small runs made in London factories. If they sold, they could then be manufactured on a mass scale. Changing styles every week and introducing bands, cafés, vintage clothing and young designers into its store, Top Shop successfully tapped into a desire to mix high street, vintage and designer in one look, rather than looking too obviously 'designer'. The look, combining high style and mass-market, is identifiably 'British', yet shows how much of what is considered to be British style is often London-oriented and London-led. Top Shop arguably revolutionised women's fashion more than the individual designers whose eclectic boutiques also characterised the city's fashion culture in the late nineties. Like the grand department stores that are its forebears (see Chapters Three and Four), the chain-store used the city's forward consumer thrust to consolidate its position as an extremely innovative retailer at the turn of the century, changing not only the fashion economy, but the London look as well.

POSTSCRIPT: BEYOND 2000 *Caroline Evans*

In September 2000 at the Grey Area at the Institute of Contemporary Arts in London, the design label nothing nothing showed a video with a triple screen which juxtaposed, on the left, rapid-fire tourist images of London with, on the right, the life of a dress and its designer in the studio. The central frame showed wire-frame architectural drawings revolving in space, onto which images from either side were periodically mapped, making an imaginative connection between the life of the city and the dress (figs. 163, 164).

nothing nothing's installation painted a picture of London fashion as pure experiment: there was literally nothing to wear (for the customer) and nothing to bank (for the company). nothing nothing started in 1998 by launching two seasons of non-existent fashion shows before, in its third season, showing in the Atlantis Gallery in Brick Lane. nothing nothing's designer, Julian Roberts, has produced clothing through a range of media: video, drawing, text and cloth. By focusing on the experience of construction, nothing nothing conceived of clothing not simply as a product to be worn, but as an object of the imagination to be dreamt up and somehow brought to life. Yet by 2004 Julian Roberts, now designing with Sophie Cheung, was showing on the official schedule during London Fashion Week.

Conceptual fashion is on the verge of trickery – it is real, but you cannot see it. Like the institution of London fashion itself, there is something definite to be exported, but so often it is an idea rather than an actual product. Its capital is thus cultural or at least symbolic as much as it is economic. Critics complain that London fashion is uncommercial and unwearable, that it is a case of the emperor's new clothes. Yet, as the past two hundred years have shown, the story of London fashion is not simply mythical; or, if it is, then it is a myth that has generated its own powerful reality.

London fashion has huge cultural capital, even where there is almost no economic capital to support it. In both Italy and the USA, fashion contributes significantly to the national economy, and in France too it is understood to be an important part of the national culture. By contrast, the British fashion industry, although by no means insignificant, was always far smaller; in recent years it has shrunk further. Patrick McCarthy, editor of America's *Women's Wear Daily*, has made the point that, in the past Britain, unlike Italy and the USA, 'just didn't have the infrastructure and the belief in fashion' to develop its industry, and its great textile companies such as Courtaulds and ICI, he argues, 'never supported fashion'.[1] But it may be this very poverty that is the motor which drives London fashion, with its 'have a go' ethic that forces young designers to extreme postures to get attention in a country that lacks an industry infrastructure. There are more young designers in London than in many other capital cities. By contrast, in other fashion capitals such as Tokyo, it is not considered acceptable to set up alone as a designer, while in continental Europe, with a more hierarchical education system, lengthy apprenticeships and a more conservative in-house ethos, it is very hard for young designers to establish themselves.

The 'have a go' mentality can be accompanied by an eager amateurism. London design companies can be characterised by chaotic production and hand-to-mouth business methods, as well as their dedication to social life and dressing up. In the late 1950s, Mary Quant, like so many who followed her, dressed in a way considered so extraordinary that business people were unimpressed and would not back her. Yet her very ignorance of the protocols of her industry gave her

Fig. 163 nothing nothing's spring/ summer 2001 collection. Video by Julian Roberts; photography by Ian Gillett. (Copyright 2001 Julian Roberts and Ian Gillett).

Fig. 164   Still from the film representing nothing nothing's spring/summer 2001 collection. Shown at London's ICA in 2000, the tripartite screen mapped fashion onto tourist imagery of London. nothing nothing's unconventional ways of showing extended from film to non-existent fashion shows. The designer behind the company, Julian Roberts, eventually put it up for sale on E-bay for £1 and reinvented the company as JULIAN AND and then as JULIAN AND SOPHIE, with Sophie Cheung. Video by Julian Roberts; photography by Ian Gillett. (Copyright 2001 Julian Roberts and Ian Gillett).

Fig. 165   Dress designed by Jonathan Saunders, spring/summer 2004. This hand-printed silk chiffon dress featured on the cover of British *Vogue* in January 2004. Saunders is a graduate of the Central Saint Martins School of Art and Design Fashion MA. He is a print designer and has a consultancy with Pucci.

the freedom to make things up as she went. Many London designers have been more interested in pursuing a vision than in building a business. Barbara Hulanicki of Biba is one such example, who would not compromise for the mass-market.

Yet, paradoxically, London produces the greatest number of trained fashion students, and they find employment worldwide. The city offers postgraduate degrees in fashion design, including those at Central Saint Martins College of Art and Design and the Royal College of Art, where the first such course in fashion design was set up in 1949. At undergraduate level too, London fashion education is unique, with courses at Kingston, Middlesex, Westminster, the Surrey Institute, Ravensbourne, London College of Fashion, and Central Saint Martins producing numerous graduates every year. London exports its design talent, not only when Paris couture houses buy in stars such as McQueen, Galliano and McCartney, but more commonly, when the nameless hundreds of graduates from the London fashion schools immediately find work in Italy, France and the USA with labels such as Versace and Donna Karan. That said, some of the city's most prominent designers, including Quant and Vivienne Westwood, have had no formal training.

In the 1960s the Royal College of Art produced most of London's fashion talent. In the 1980s much of it came from St Martin's and, in the 1990s, the renamed Central Saint Martins. Both were, and are, art colleges teaching a range of courses alongside fashion, from fine art to graphics, and this cross-fertilisation and the art school ethos have something to do with the attitude that characterises London graduates. Looking back on his career, the stylist Judy Blame said:

> I do jump around – I jump from fashion to music to whatever, and that's what keeps it fresh for me after doing it for over twenty years now. I'm not just in the fashion business, you didn't channel it in one direction, you left yourself open to experiment with lots of different types of media. And then you learn ways of mixing them back in together. When I was doing some of my first shoots for *i-D*, I was taking something that wasn't a fashion idea, but whacking it through a fashion editorial. There was one I did on pollution, one on recycling.[2]

This is an approach that is highly characteristic of London, and it shows, for example, in the editorial policy of *Nova*, or the pop, fashion and graphics interfaces of the 1960s. If it is a defining feature of London fashion, it is a highly original one, but one that is not necessarily commercial, and does not always translate for the mass-market. It can entertain and inspire, it can be exported as an idea, but it is not a model for business and sales. Judy Blame's attitude sums it up: 'I don't see why I have to do one [fashion editorial] every month just to get an advertising job and then style some dodgy shoot in Milan. For loads of money. And then just kiss arse. It just doesn't suit me. I don't see the value in it.'[3]

Blame describes how many prestigious London stylists, photographers, hair and make-up

artists make their living from jobs they are not especially proud of, and their reputations from ones of which they are. This is the singular economy of London where people are prepared to work for nothing, partly for creative independence, partly in order to generate the buzz that will secure them lucrative contracts in New York or Milan. Influential stylists like Katie Grand started in London before moving to international brands such as Prada (frequently while continuing to live in London). And fashion professionals in New York and Milan read the London fashion press to find out who is making waves.

Established professionals who command enormous fees internationally may still stay loyal to their roots and work for nothing for small London enterprises. The photographer Nick Knight moves between doing an international Dior advertising campaign one week and a fashion story for *i-D* magazine the next. This loyalty to where people started means that London fashion professionals often work in loose networks. These networks may cross over disciplines fruitfully. When the artist Wolfgang Tillmans won the prestigious Turner Prize for art in 2000, he included his earlier fashion shoots for *i-D* in the Turner exhibition at the Tate. This artistic cross-fertilisation operates in both directions, as when the London magazine *Dazed & Confused* opened an art gallery, or reproduced the work of contemporary artists in the magazine pages. Pop music too, so dominated by Britain and America in the post-war period, plays a similar part in the new culture of fashion. Bands go on tour wearing spectacular clothes and so disseminate a 'look' abroad, outside the usual fashion industry networks. The London look can, in an age of media overdrive, quickly become an international one.

What are the defining characteristics of London fashion? The city thrives on a longstanding dialectic between tradition and innovation, producing both alternative styles and hybrid fashions that range from polyglot fusions to fine tailoring with a subtle twist. The liveliness of London fashion emerges from its history of quirky little shops rather than big design labels; a cultural mix that has moved during the centuries from imperial transaction to present-day immigration; the crossover between fashion, art, architecture and music; and a strong sense of a past ever-ripe for playful reworking and reconfiguring. The London look might best be summed up as an edgy, of-the-moment 'have a go' mentality not seen in other fashion capitals, a spirit that has fed everything from technological innovation and changing working practices in the nineteenth century to the unsubsidised splendour of fashion spectaculars at the end of the twentieth. And London's influence is palpable. The London fashion press is read worldwide; there is more fashion editorial in British newspapers than most; its art-school fashion graduates work across the globe; the city has a unique tradition of outstanding subcultures, and the street wields as much influence as the catwalk. The very idea of London fashion is strong and compelling, possibly because it constantly eludes definition, is constantly on the run. This international idea of a London look does have its drawbacks. The 'edge' people associate with London can be restrictive. Plenty of designers are commercially successful and well respected, but do not receive the same publicity as their more radical colleagues, especially when London's influence is so disproportionately large, so highly visible.[4] What often gets press, to the detriment of more conventional designers, is what fits with an idea of London fashion.

Will there be a role for London fashion in the future? Undoubtedly. London fashion at its most uncompromising will always find a niche, as will its social impact and cultural imperative.

NOTES

INTRODUCTION

1. The history of fashion in its metropolitan context is discussed in Christopher Breward, *Fashion* (Oxford: Oxford University Press, 2003), pp. 169–215 and David Gilbert, 'Urban Outfitting' in Stella Bruzzi and Pamela Church Gibson, eds, *Fashion Cultures: Theories, Explorations and Analysis* (London: Routledge, 2000), pp. 7–24.
2. For an overview of the rise of Paris to fashion prominence, see Valerie Steele, *Paris Fashion: A Cultural History* (New York: Oxford University Press, 1988).
3. For a summary of the production and promotion of New York fashion, see Caroline Rennolds Milbank, *New York Fashion: The Evolution of American Style* (New York: Abrams, 1989).
4. For Milan as a fashion centre see Giannino Malossi, ed., *Volare: The Icon of Italy in Global Pop Culture* (New York: Monacelli Press, 1999) and Nicola White, *Reconstructing Italian Fashion: America and the Development of the Italian Fashion Industry* (Oxford: Berg, 2000). For Tokyo, see Leonard Kohen, *New Fashion Japan* (Tokyo: Kodansha, 1984) and Soichi Aoki, *Fruits* (London: Phaidon, 2001).
5. Previous coverage of London's status as a fashion city includes Christopher Breward, *Fashioning London: Clothing and the Modern Metropolis* (Oxford: Berg, 2004) and Andrew Tucker, *The London Fashion Book* (London: Thames & Hudson, 1998).
6. Francis Sheppard, *London: A History* (Oxford: Oxford University Press, 1998), p. 142.
7. For accounts of London's fashion cultures from the sixteenth to the eighteenth centuries, see Jane Ashelford, *Dress in the Age of Elizabeth I* (London: Batsford, 1988); Miles Ogborn, *Spaces of Modernity: London's Geographies 1680–1780* (New York, Guilford Press, 1998); Liza Picard, *Restoration London* (London: Weidenfeld & Nicolson, 1997); and Aileen Ribeiro, *The Art of Dress: Fashion in England and France 1750–1820* (New Haven and London: Yale University Press, 1998).
8. Sheppard, p. 130.

9. Sophie von la Roche, quoted in Peter Thorold, *The London Rich: The Creation of a Great City from 1666 to the Present* (London: Viking, 1999), p. 126.

CHAPTER 1: Gentlefolk in Town 1800–30

1. Marquis de Vermont and Sir Charles Darnley, *London and Paris, or Comparative Sketches* (London: Longman, 1823), pp. 31–2.
2. Roy Porter, *London: A Social History* (London: Hamish Hamilton, 1994), pp. 180–4.
3. The classic account of the development of the West End remains John Summerson, *Georgian London* (London: Pelican, 1962), pp. 18–22.
4. Alison Adburgham, *Shops and Shopping 1800–1914* (London: Barrie & Jenkins, 1989), p. 108.
5. Jane Rendell, 'Subjective Space: An Architectural History of the Burlington Arcade' in Duncan McCorquodale, Katerina Ruedi and Sarah Wigglesworth, eds, *Desiring Practices* (London: Black Dog, 1996), pp. 216–33.
6. See H. B. Wheatley, *Bond Street Old and New 1686–1911* (London: Fine Art Society, 1911).
7. Frank Whitbourn, *Mr Lock of St James Street* (London: Heinemann, 1971), pp. 60–3.
8. See R. Walker, *The Savile Row Story* (London: Prion, 1988) for the early history and later development of Savile Row.
9. Alison Adburgham, *Silver Fork Society: Fashionable Life and Literature from 1814–1840* (London: Constable, 1983), p. 60.
10. Pierce Egan, *Life in London* (London: Sherwood, Neely & Jones, 1821), pp. 23–4.
11. Aileen Ribeiro, *The Art of Dress: Fashion in England and France* (New Haven and London: Yale University Press, 1998), pp. 104–5.
12. Egan, p. 146.
13. Captain Jesse, *The Life of George Brummell Esq., Vol 1* (London: John Nimmo, 1886), pp. 62–3.
14. Anon, *Portraits from Life or Memoirs of a Rambler* (London: J. Moore, 1800), p. 56.
15. See Diana Donald, *The Age of Caricature: Satirical Prints in the Reign of George III* (New

Haven and London: Yale University Press, 1996).
16. Kay Staniland, *In Royal Fashion: The Clothes of Princess Charlotte of Wales and Queen Victoria 1796–1901* (London: Museum of London, 1997), p. 49.
17. Penelope Byrde, *Jane Austen Fashion: Fashion and Needlework in the Works of Jane Austen* (Ludlow: Excellent Press, 1999), pp. 54–69.
18. Mary Cathcart Borer, *An Illustrated Guide to London 1800* (London: Hale, 1988), p. 94.
19. Byrde, pp. 70–2.
20. Adburgham, *Shops and Shopping*, pp. 8–9.
21. See Christopher Breward, *Fashion* (Oxford: Oxford University Press, 2003), pp. 116–20.
22. Peter Thorold, *The London Rich: The Creation of a Great City from 1666 to the Present* (London: Viking, 1999), p. 239.
23. Jane Rendell, *The Pursuit of Pleasure: Gender, Space and Architecture in Regency London* (London: Athlone Press, 2002), pp. 86–103.
24. Amanda Vickery, *The Gentleman's Daughter: Women's Lives in Georgian England* (New Haven and London: Yale University Press, 1998), pp. 240–50.
25. Egan, p. 239.
26. Pierce Egan, *Boxiana or Sketches of Ancient and Modern Pugilism* (London: Folio Society, 1976), p. 133.
27. Egan, *Boxiana*, pp. 159–60.
28. Bernard Blackmantle, *The English Spy* (London: Sherwood, Gilbert & Piper, 1826), vol. 1, p. 166.

CHAPTER 2: Clothing a World City 1830–60

1. The sale took place at Mr Phillips' rooms at 73 New Bond Street on 15–17 December 1830. A catalogue of the sales on 16 and 17 December, which comprised 'a portion of the expensive wardrobe, military jackets and splendid silk and velvet robes, plumes of ostrich feathers and miscellaneous items [of the] late His Majesty George the Fourth's' is held at the Museum of London [MoL 38.294/1].

2. Anon, *The Whole Art of Dress or The Road to Elegance and Fashion at the Enormous Saving of 30%*, (London: Effingham Wilson, 1830), pp. 5–6.

3. For detailed studies of these two firms, see Pamela Sharpe, ' "Cheapness and Economy": Manufacturing and Retailing Ready-made Clothing in London and Essex, 1830–1850', *Textile History* 26 (2), 1995, pp. 203–13 and Stanley Chapman, 'The Innovating Entrepreneurs in the British Ready-made Clothing Industry', *Textile History* 24 (1), 1993, pp. 5–25.

4. MoL Tradecards 37A: E. Moses & Son, 154 Minories & 86 Aldgate, 1846.

5. L. Hyam & Company, *The Quarterly Mirror*, Autumn/Winter 1852, p. 3.

6. MoL 76.77/6c: L. Hyam, 36 Gracechurch Street, c.1844.

7. Katrina Honeyman, *Well Suited: A History of the Leeds Clothing Industry 1850–1900* (Oxford: Oxford University Press, 2000), pp. 112–13, n. 26.

8. John Fisher Murray, *The World of London* (London: Richard Bentley, 1845), vol. 1, p. 171.

9. MoL Tradecards 214: Samuel Brothers, Merchant Tailors & Outfitters, 29 Ludgate Hill, c.1851.

10. MoL Tradecards 37A: see above.

11. J. Stirling Coyne, 'I'm a gent – I'm a gent', c.1855 [Reading University Library: Spellman Collection of Victorian Music Covers].

12. David M. Evans, *City Men and City Manners* (London: Groombridge & Sons, 1852), p. 166. See also Edgar Allan Poe, *Poetry and Tales* (New York, 1984), pp. 388–90, quoted in David Kynaston, *The City of London: A World of Its Own 1815–1890*, (London: Chatto & Windus, 1994), vol. 1, pp. 113–14.

13. George Augustus Sala, *Twice Around the Clock* (London: Houlston & Wright, 1859), p. 195.

14. Sala, p. 83. 15. Evans, pp. 153–4.

16. Sarah Levitt, *Victorians Unbuttoned: Registered Designs for Clothing, Their Makers and Wearers, 1839–1900* (London: George Allen & Unwin, 1986), p. 53, fig. 5; MoL Z982, Z984, Ford's Fashions, 1861.

17. MoL Z982, Z984: see above.

18. Alison Adburgham, *Shops and Shopping 1800–1914* (London: George Allen & Unwin, 1981), pp. 142–3.

19. MoL 65.17/1. The woven label reads 'PETER ROBINSON/MANTLE MANUFACTURER/103 TO 108 OXFORD STREET'.

20. Ralph Hyde and Valerie Cumming, 'The Prints of Benjamin Read, Tailor and Print Maker', *Print Quarterly*, 17 (3), 2000, p. 267.

21. Albert Smith, *The Natural History of the Gent* (London: David Bogue, 1847), p. 12.

22. 'Critical Observations on Gentlemen's Fashions for May, 1828', *The Gentleman's Magazine of Fashions, Fancy Costumes and the Regimentals of the Army*, May 1828, p. 5.

23. Philippe Perrot, transl. Richard Bienvenu, *Fashioning the Bourgeoisie: A History of Clothing in the Nineteenth Century*, (New Jersey: Princeton University Press, 1994), p. 40.

24. Alison Adburgham, *Women in Print: Writing Women and Women's Magazines from the Restoration to the Accession of Victoria* (London: George Allen & Unwin, 1972), p. 230.

25. Sala, pp. 199–200.

26. Patrick Jackson, ' "Skittles" and the Marquis: A Victorian Love Affair', *History Today*, December 1995, pp. 47–52.

27. W. P. Frith, *My Autobiography and Reminiscences* (London: Richard Bentley & Son, 1887), vol. 1, pp. 278–80.

28. Max Schlesinger, *Saunterings in and about London* (London: Nathaniel Cooke, 1853), p. 106.

29. Madeleine Ginsburg, 'The Young Queen and Her Clothes' in *Early Victorian Costume 1830–1860* (London: V & A Museum for the Costume Society, 1969), p. 42.

30. Almanach du Commerce de Paris: H. Creed et Cie, tailleurs, 59 rue Neuve St Augustin, 1870.

31. Elizabeth Ann Coleman, *The Opulent Era: Fashions of Worth, Doucet and Pingat* (New York: Thames & Hudson, 1989), pp. 9, 33.

32. Queen Victoria , *Leaves from a Journal* (London: André Deutsch, 1961), p. 60.

33. Kay Staniland, *In Royal Fashion: The Clothes of Princess Charlotte of Wales and Queen Victoria 1796–1901*, (London: Museum of London, 1997), pp. 86, 131–5, 144–5.

34. MoL Tradecards 231: E. Moses & Son, *The Desideratum*, 1851.

35. Murray, pp. 186–7.

36. Anon, *London As It Is To-Day* (London: G. Clarke & Company, 1851), p. 403; Schlesinger, pp. 16–18.

37. Trudy Bliss, *Jane Welsh Carlyle: A New Selection of Her Letters* (London: Gollancz, 1949) p. 282.

CHAPTER 3: Fashion in the Age of Imperialism 1860–90

1. Gustave Doré and Blanchard Jerrold, *London: A Pilgrimage* (New York: Dover, 1970), pp. 35–6.

2. See Henry Mayhew, *London Labour and the London Poor* (London: Griffin, Bohn & Co., 1851); Charles Dickens, *Our Mutual Friend* (London: Chapman & Hall, 1864); George Gissing, *In the Year of Jubilee* (London: Lawrence & Bullen, 1891); Charles Booth, *Life and Labour of the People in London* (London: Macmillan, 1897).

3. *Collins' Illustrated Guide to London* (London: William Collins, 1877), pp. 113–14.

4. See James Schmiechen, *Sweated Industries and Sweated Labour: The London Clothing Trades 1860–1914* (Urbana: University of Illinois Press, 1984).

5. Francis Sheppard, *London: A History* (Oxford: Oxford University Press, 1998), p. 311.

6. Christina Walkley, *The Ghost in the Looking Glass: The Victorian Seamstress* (London: Peter Owen, 1981), p. 36.

7. Walkley, pp. 53–4.

8. Stephen Howarth, *Henry Poole, Founders of Savile Row, The Making of a Legend* (Honiton: Bene Factum Publishing, 2003), pp. 78–9.

9. Christopher Breward, *The Hidden Consumer: Masculinities, Fashion and City Life 1860–1914* (Manchester: Manchester University Press, 1999), pp. 106–7.

10. See Thomas Richards, *The Commodity Culture of Victorian England: Advertising and Spectacle 1851–1914* (London: Verso, 1991).

11. Albert Smith, ed., *Sketches of London Life and Character* (London: James Blackwood & Co., 1870), p. 117.

12. Erika Rappaport, *Shopping for Pleasure: Women in the Making of London's West End* (Princeton: Princeton University Press, 2000), pp. 16–47.

13. Alison Adburgham, *Shops and Shopping 1800–1914* (London: Barrie & Jenkins, 1989), p. 156.

14. Adburgham, pp. 220–3. See also Lou Taylor 'Wool Cloth and Gender: The Use of Woollen Cloth in Women's Dress in Britain, 1865–85' in Amy de la Haye and Elizabeth Wilson, eds, *Defining Dress: Dress as Object, Meaning and Identity* (Manchester: Manchester University Press, 1999), pp. 30–47.

15. Alison Adburgham, *Liberty's: A Biography of a Shop* (London: George Allen & Unwin, 1975), pp. 51–2.

16. Daniel Kirwan, *Palace and Hovel or Phases of London Life* (Hartford: Bellknap and Bliss, 1871), pp. 140–1.

17. Leonore Davidoff, *The Best Circles: Society Etiquette and the Season* (London: Croom Helm, 1973), pp. 28–9.

18. The 'upper ten' was a colloquial term for the upper ten thousand: the most prominent members of a population. It was first coined in the United States in the 1840s, but by the 1880s was being used by journals such as *Punch* and *The Queen* in reference to the membership and activities of London Society.

19. Cited in Christopher Breward, *The Hidden Consumer: Masculinities, Fashion and City Life 1860–1914* (Manchester: Manchester University Press, 1999), p. 46.

20. See *Simply Stunning: The Pre-Raphaelite Art of Dressing* (Cheltenham: Cheltenham Art Gallery, 1996).

21. See Stella Mary Newton, *Health, Art & Reason: Dress Reformers of the Nineteenth Century* (London: John Murray, 1974).

22. Cited in Christopher Breward, *The Culture of Fashion* (Manchester: Manchester University Press, 1995), p. 163.

CHAPTER 4: Popular Dressing 1890–1914

1. Francis Sheppard, *London: A History* (Oxford: Oxford University Press, 1998), pp. 313–14.

2. E. T. Cook, *Highways and Byways in London* (London: Macmillan, 1902), pp. 298–9.

3. Thomas Burke, *The Streets of London* (London: Batsford, 1940), p. 145.

4. Erika Rappaport, *Shopping for Pleasure: Women in the Making of London's West End* (Princeton: Princeton University Press, 2000), pp. 160–5.

5. Thomas Burke, *Nights in Town: A London Autobiography* (London: Allen & Unwin, 1915), p. 397.

6. Lou Taylor, 'The Wardrobe of Mrs Leonard Messel' in Christopher Breward, Becky Conekin and Caroline Cox, eds, *The Englishness of English Dress* (Oxford: Berg, 2002), pp. 121–2. The Messel collection is held by Brighton Museum and Art Gallery.

7. Deborah Cherry & Jane Beckett, eds, *The Edwardian Era* (London: Barbican Art Gallery, 1987), pp. 71–3.

8. Angela McRobbie, *British Fashion Design: Rag Trade or Image Industry* (London: Routledge, 1998), pp. 28–9. See also Helen Reynolds, *Couture or Trade* (Chichester: Phillimore & Co., 1997).

9. Mario Borsa, *The English Stage of Today* (London: John Lane, 1908), p. 7.

10. E. Short, *Fifty Years of Vaudeville* (London: Eyre & Spottiswoode, 1946), p. 43.

11. R. Mander and J. Mitchenson, *Musical Comedy: A Story in Pictures* (London: Peter Davies, 1969), p.13.

12. Peter Bailey, 'Naughty but Nice: Musical Comedy and the Rhetoric of the Girl 1892–1914' in M. Booth & J. Kaplan, eds, *The Edwardian Theatre: Essays in Performance and the Stage* (Cambridge: Cambridge University Press, 1996), pp. 39–40.

13. Lady Wyndham, *Charles Wyndham and Mary Moore* (London: [private printing] 1925), p. 242.

14. Wyndham, p. 247.

15. Wyndham, p. 242.

16. MoL 28.125/1.

17. Lady Duff Gordon, *Discretions and Indiscretions* (London: Jarrolds, 1932), p. 65. See also M. Etherington Smith and J. Pilcher, *The It Girls* (London: Hamish Hamilton, 1986) and J. Kaplan and S. Stowell,

Theatre and Fashion: Oscar Wilde to the Suffragettes (Cambridge: Cambridge University Press, 1994).

18. Edwin Pugh, *The City of the World: A Book about London and the Londoner* (London: Thomas Nelson, 1908), pp. 41–3.

19. Percy Fitzgerald, *Music Hall Land* (London: Ward & Downey, 1890), p. 4.

20. Rappaport, p. 219. See also Lisa Tickner, *The Spectacle of Women: Imagery of the Suffrage Campaign, 1907–1914* (Chicago: University of Chicago Press, 1988).

CHAPTER 5: Glamorous Modernity 1914–30

1. Natacha Rambova, *Rudy: An Intimate Portrait of Rudolph Valentino by his wife Natacha Rambova* (London: Hutchinson & Co Ltd, 1926), p. 74.

2. 'The Society Gypsies', *British Vogue*, 13 June 1928, p. 45.

3. Barbara Cartland, *The Isthmus Years 1919–1939* (London: Hutchinson & Co. Ltd, 1943), p. 12.

4. 'Fashion And The Fashion Makers', *British Vogue*, Late March 1922, p. 53.

5. Norman Hartnell, *Silver and Gold* (London: Evans Brothers, 1955), p. 14.

6. Isobel (Mrs Nathan), Rejected script for a BBC broadcast, 1928, AAD/1991/12/7/1. See also Board of Education, 'Design and the Cotton Industry' (London: HMSO, 1929), p. 10, quoted in Emily Baines, 'Innovation and Fashion Leadership: Studio Design in the Interwar Printed Textiles Industry', *Text* 31, 2003/04, p. 39.

7. 'All Things to All Women', *British Vogue*, Early May 1923, p. 31.

8. 'Vogue at the London Collections', *British Vogue*, 3 October 1928, p. 57.

9. Hubert Llewellyn Smith, ed., *The New Survey of London Life and Labour*, 9 volumes (London: P. S. King & Son Ltd, 1930–35), vol. 2, p. 305.

10. 'Isobel', *Eve's Film Review* 578, 30 June 1932.

11. Jenny Hammerton, *For Ladies Only? Eve's Film Review Pathé Cinemagazine 1921–1933* (Hastings: The Projection Box, 2001), pp. 75–8.

12. 'Fashion Chance for Women', *Daily Mirror*, 21 May 1932, AAD/1991/12/5/4 and Helen Burke 'Mainly Women', *Sunday Pictorial*, 22 May 1932, AAD/1991/12/5/5.

13. 'Vogue at the London Collections', p. 59.

14. 'Does Paris Lead? British Designers' Challenge to France', *The Bystander*, 4 September 1929, pp. 518–19.

15. Hartnell, p. 30.

16. Cecil Beaton, *The Glass of Fashion* (London: Weidenfeld & Nicolson, 1954), p. 42.

17. 'The Truth Game', *The Theatre World*, November 1928, p. 16.

18. 'The Well-Dressed Actress', *British Vogue*, 28 November 1928, p. 77.

19. 'The Vogue for Shopkeeping', *British Vogue*, 28 May 1930, pp. 82–3.

20. Eileen Hunter, *The Russell Case and After* (London: André Deutsch, 1973), pp.37, 53.

21. MoL 68.143a-b. For a photograph of Hilda Moore wearing the outfit, see 'Interference', *The Theatre World*, March 1927, p. 22.

22. 'London-Made Fashions', *British Vogue*, 10 October 1929, pp. 45–6.

23. Llewellyn Smith, vol. 2, pp. 298, 315.

24. Alexandre Vassiliev, *Beauty in Exile* (New York: Harry N. Abrams, Inc., 2000), pp. 194, 224–31.

25. 'Round the Dress Shows', *Mabs Fashions*, February 1927, p. 18.

26. Jan and Cora Gordon, *The London Roundabout* (London: George G. Harrap & Co. Ltd, 1933), p. 199.

27. Gordon, pp. 200–1.

28. Helen Reynolds, *Couture or Trade: An Early Pictorial Record of the London College of Fashion* (Chichester: Phillimore & Co. Ltd, 1997), pp. xiii–xvii, xxiv.

29. Llewellyn Smith, vol. 2, p. 297 (statistics include those working in the underclothing trade), p. 301.

30. Amy de la Haye, 'The Dissemination of Design from Haute Couture to Fashionable Ready-to-Wear during the 1920s', *Textile History*, 24 (1), 1993, pp. 39–40.

31. Llewellyn Smith, vol. 8, pp. 275–7, 281, 311.

32. Victor Macclure, *How To Be Happy in London* (London: Arrowsmith, 1926), pp. 105, 164.

33. The Hon. Mrs. C. W. Forester, *Success Through Dress* (London: Duckworth, 1925), pp. 17, 22, 26–7.

34. Mary Scott, *Women Talking. An Anthology from The Guardian Women's Pages* (London: Pandora, 1987), p. 119.

35. W. L. George, *A London Mosaic* (London: W. Collins Sons & Co. Ltd, 1921), pp. 71–2.

36. E. Beresford Chancellor, *Liberty and Regent Street* (London: Liberty & Co. Ltd, [c.1926]), p. 12.

37. MoL 82.724/1: Liberty & Co. Ltd dress catalogue, autumn 1925.

38. Victoria & Albert Museum, *Liberty's 1875–1975* (London: HMSO, 1975), p. 39: C22, C24.

39. 'An Oriental Fantasy by Dove', *British Vogue*, Early October 1925, p. 87.

40. Hazel Clark, 'Modern Textiles 1926–1939', *The Journal of the Decorative Arts Society* 12, 1988, p. 49.

41. Llewellyn Smith, vol. 2, p. 288.

42. Paul Morand, *A Frenchman's London* (London: Cassell & Co. Ltd, 1934), pp. 76–7.

43. Macclure, p. 145.

CHAPTER 6: Broken Traditions 1930–55

1. 'What London Shows', *British Vogue*, 2 April 1930, p. 47.
2. 'Window Display. A Revolution in Savile Row', *The Tailor & Cutter*, 27 February 1931, p. 201.
3. 'Start of London Season', *The Tailor & Cutter*, 15 May 1931, p. 385.
4. Thelma Benjamin, *London Shops and Shopping* (London: Herbert Joseph Ltd, 1934), p. 70.
5. 'Stealing His Stuff', *British Vogue*, 19 September 1928, pp. 72, 84.
6. Katrina Honeyman, *Well Suited: A History of the Leeds Clothing Industry 1850–1900* (Oxford: Oxford University Press, 2000), pp. 260–1.
7. Benjamin, pp. 79–80; Cathy Ross, *Twenties London: A City in the Jazz Age* (London: Philip Wilson, 2003), p. 68.
8. David Wainwright, *The British Tradition: Simpson – A World of Style* (London: Quiller Press, 1996), p. 6.
9. Wainwright, p. 10.
10. Paul Morand, *A Frenchman's London* (London: Cassell & Co. Ltd, 1934), pp. 169–70.
11. Richard Calvocoressi, 'Ashley's Textiles', *Journal of the Decorative Arts Society* 3, 1978, p. 5.
12. DAKS/Simpson Archive, 'Press Cuttings 1936', no title, *Advertisers Weekly*, 7 May 1936.
13. Thomas Burke, *London In My Time* (London: Rich & Cowan Ltd, 1934), pp. 228–9.
14. John Compton, 'The Night Architecture of the Thirties', *Journal of the Decorative Art Society* 4, 1979, pp. 44, 47.
15. G. W. Stonier, *Round London With the Unicorn* (London: Turnstile Press, 1951), p. 15.
16. Nigel Gray, *The Worst of Times: An Oral History of the Great Depression in Britain* (London: Wildwood House, 1985), pp. 66, 69.
17. Jan and Cora Gordon, *The London Roundabout* (London: George G. Harrap & Co. Ltd, 1933), pp. 204–5.
18. MoL 96.97a-b; 96.98. Islington and Hackney Museums have garments made by Mrs Lipley.
19. Sally Alexander, 'Becoming a Woman in London in the 1920s and 1930s' in David Feldman and Gareth Stedman Jones, eds, *Metropolis London: Histories and Representations since 1800* (London & New York: Routledge, 1989), pp. 252, 264.
20. Gordon, p. 132.
21. Burke, pp. 30, 68.
22. 'Film and Clothes', *The Tailor & Cutter*, 25 January 1935, p. 67.
23. MoL 77.89/137: *Trocadero Magazine*, January 1931.
24. 'London Launches a Mode', *British Vogue*, 23 January 1935, pp. 43–5, 82, 84, 86.
25. Frank Burlington Fawcett, ed., *Their Majesties' Courts Held at Buckingham Palace 1932* (London: Grayson & Grayson, 1932), p. 93.
26. Norman Hartnell, *Silver and Gold* (London: Evans Brothers, 1955), p. 49.
27. Leonard Mosley, *Backs to the Wall: London Under Fire 1939–1945* (London: Weidenfeld & Nicolson, 1971), pp. 188–91.
28. For a detailed analysis of the government's strategy, see Christopher Sladen, *The Conscription of Fashion: Utility Cloth, Clothing and Footwear 1941–1952* (Aldershot: Scolar Press, 1995).
29. Amy de la Haye, ed., *The Cutting Edge: Fifty years of British Fashion 1947–1997* (London: V & A Publications, 1998), p. 16.
30. Ann Scott-James, 'Austerity Clothes for the Fourth Year of the War', *Picture Post*, 29 August 1942, p. 23.
31. 'Women's Fashions, 1942–1943: Mass-Produced Utility Models', *The Illustrated London News*, 3 October 1942, p. 387.
32. Edna McKenna, 'Verdict on the Fashion Shows', *Daily Graphic*, 28 January 1950.
33. Pamela Berry, 'A Phoenix Rises Out of Sackcloth and Ashes', *The Tailor & Cutter*, 18 March 1955, pp. 326–7.
34. William Sanson, 'A Public for Jive' in A. G. Weidenfeld, ed., *The Public's Progress* (London: Contact Publications Ltd, 1947), pp. 56, 61.
35. Nik Cohn, *Today There Are No Gentlemen* (London: Weidenfeld & Nicolson, 1971), p. 30.

CHAPTER 7: Post-war Poses 1955–75

1. *Time*, 15 April 1966, p. 32.
2. See Sarah Thornton, *Club Cultures: Music, Media and Subcultural Capital* (Cambridge: Polity, 1995).
3. Mary Quant, *Quant by Quant* (London: Cassell, 1966), p. 43.
4. Quant, p. 35.
5. Quant, pp. 34–5.
6. Paul Gorman, *The Look: Adventures in Pop and Rock Fashion* (London: Sanctuary Publishing, 2001), p. 48.
7. Gorman, p. 28.
8. Hardy Amies, *The Englishman's Suit*, cited in Gorman, p. 28.
9. George Melly, *Revolt into Style: The Pop Arts in Britain* (London: Allen Lane, 1970), p. 150.
10. Colin MacInnes, *Absolute Beginners* (Harmondsworth: Penguin, [1959] 1964), pp. 70–1.
11. A brilliant survey of Mod styles in both central and suburban London over almost a decade is in Gorman, pp. 51–63.
12. Dick Hebdige went so far as to argue that 'all post-war British youth culture must be reinterpreted as a succession of differential responses to the black immigrant presence in Britain from the 1950s onward'. See *Subculture: The Meaning of Style* (London: Methuen, 1979), p. 29.
13. Juliet Gardiner, *From the Bomb to the Beatles: The Changing Face of Post-war Britain* (London: Collins & Brown, 1999), pp. 137–8.
14. Alexandra Pringle, 'Chelsea Girl' in Sara Maitland, ed., *Very Heaven: Looking Back at the 1960s* (London: Virago, 1988), pp. 37–8.
15. Gorman, p. 45.
16. Jonathan Aitken, *The Young Meteors* (London: Secker & Warburg, 1967), p. 34.
17. Pringle, p. 39.
18. Brigid Keenan, *The Women We Wanted to Look Like* (London: Macmillan, 1977), p. 100.
19. Pringle, p. 39.
20. Jon Savage, *England's Dreaming: Sex Pistols and Punk Rock* (London: Faber & Faber, 1991), p. 5.
21. Marnie Fogg, *Boutique: A '60s Cultural Phenomenon* (London: Mitchell Beazley, 2003), p. 175.
22. Joel Lobenthal, *Radical Rags: Fashions of the Sixties* (New York: Abbeville Press, 1990), p. 148.
23. Fogg, p. 70.
24. Felicity Green in the *Daily Mirror*, August 1967, quoted in Lobenthal, p. 35.
25. See Tom Wolfe, *Radical Chic & Mau-Mauing the Flak Catchers* (London: Bantam, 1971).
26. Pringle, p. 39.
27. Nik Cohn, *Today There are No Gentlemen* (London: Weidenfeld & Nicolson, 1971), p. 99.
28. Angela Carter, 'Notes for a Theory of Sixties Style' *New Society*, 1967; repr. in *Nothing Sacred: Selected Writings* (London: Virago, 1982, rev. 1992), pp. 85–90.
29. Carter, p. 87.
30. Carter, pp. 87–8. See also Harriet Vyner, *Groovy Bob: The Life and Times of Robert Fraser* (London: Faber & Faber, 1999), pp. 162–203.
31. Gorman, p. 110.

CHAPTER 8: Cultural Capital 1976–2000

1. John Ingham, *Sounds*, 9 October 1976, reprinted in Hanif Kureshi & Jon Savage, eds, *The Faber Book of Pop* (London: Faber & Faber, 1995), pp. 494–5.
2. Jon Savage, *England's Dreaming: Sex Pistols and Punk Rock* (London: Faber & Faber, 1991), p. 186. Savage's exhaustive account of London punk includes a wealth of detail about fashion and clothes worn by the participants, as well as detailing Westwood and McLaren's shop interiors and clothing designs, many of which are to be seen in the book's photographs.
3. Paul Gorman, *The Look: Adventures in Pop and Rock Fashion* (London: Sanctuary Publishing, 2001), p. 116.

4. *Sniffin' Glue* 4, 1976. No page numbers. Thanks to Roger Sabin for his help with this reference.

5. They are described succinctly in Gorman, pp. 121–2.

6. Peter York, 'The Post-Punk Mortem', *Harpers & Queen*, July 1977; repr. in *Style Wars* (London: Sidgwick & Jackson, 1980), p. 130.

7. Gorman, p. 131 and York, p. 129.

8. Carol Tulloch, 'Rebel Without a Pause: Black Street Style and Black Designers' in Juliet Ash and Elizabeth Wilson, eds, *Chic Thrills: A Fashion Reader* (London: Pandora, 1992), pp. 84–98.

9. Mark Hooper, 'Interview with Judy Blame', *032c* [Berlin] Winter 2003/04, p. 88.

10. Hooper, p. 89.

11. Terry Jones, ed., *Not Another Punk Book!,* text by Isabelle Anscombe (London: Aurum Press, 1978).

12. See Juliet Ash, 'Philosophy on the Catwalk: The Making and Wearing of Vivienne Westwood's Clothes' in Ash and Wilson, p. 169.

13. Stevie Stewart, 'Mapping the Future: Talking 'bout my Generation' in Lorraine Johnston, ed., *The Fashion Year*, vol. 3 (London: Zomba Books, 1985), p. 104.

14. Judy Blame also remembers the excitement of *The Face* and the Buffalo imagery styled by Ray Petri, pointing again to the interface of music and fashion, and the way they came together in London clubs in the eighties. See Hooper, p. 90.

15. Fiona Russell Powell, 'Dayglo Crazies, Rhinestone Rentboys, and the Glittergang' in Emily White, ed., *The Fashion Year*, vol. 2 (London: Zomba Books, 1984), p. 152.

16. Robert Violette, ed., *Leigh Bowery* (London: Violette Editions, 1998), p. 16. Bowery's poses are well documented in pictures in Violette's book. See also Sue Tilley, *Leigh Bowery: The Life and Times of an Icon* (London: Hodder & Stoughton, 1997), pp. 215–18 and Vaughan Toulouse, 'Clubbed to Death: Why be In When You Could be Out', *The Fashion Year*, vol. 3, p. 60.

17. Rebecca Arnold, 'Vivienne Westwood's Anglomania' in Christopher Breward, Becky Conekin & Caroline Cox, eds, *The Englishness of English Dress* (Oxford: Berg, 2002), pp. 161–72.

18. Kevin Davey, *English Imaginaries: Six Studies in Anglo-British Modernity* (London: Lawrence & Wishart, 1999), p. 121.

19. See Frank Mort, *Cultures of Consumption: Masculinities and Social Space in Late Twentieth-century Britain* (London: Routledge, 1996).

20. Colin McDowell, *Galliano* (London: Weidenfeld & Nicolson, 1997), pp. 70–105.

21. Quoted in Stephen Todd, 'The Importance of Being English', *Blueprint*, March 1997, p. 42.

22. Documented at the time by Andrew Tucker, *The London Fashion Book* (London: Thames & Hudson, 1998).

23. Quoted in Hilton Als, 'Gear: Postcard from London', *The New Yorker,* 17 March 1997, p. 92.

24. In *Britain*™: *Renewing our Identity* (1998), Demos argued that, as a post-industrial nation, British talent lay in the creative and service industries, identifying the UK as a 'powerhouse of ideas.' The phrase was taken up in a Department for Trade and Industry exhibition in April 1998, *powerhouse::uk*, that brought together fashion, graphics and design to represent the new fusion.

25. Mark Lennard, 'It's Not Just Ice-cream' and 'A Brief History of Cool Britannia', *New Statesman*, 3 July 1998.

26. Penny Martin, 'English-style Photography?' in Breward et al., p. 185.

27. Thanks to Carol Tulloch for this point.

POSTSCRIPT: Beyond 2000

1. Quoted in John Andrews, 'Fashion's Favorite: Which Centre Takes the Crown?' in 'Rags and Riches: A Survey of Fashion', *The Economist*, 6 March 2004, p. 4.

2. Mark Hooper, 'Interview with Judy Blame', *032c* [Berlin] Winter 2003/04, p. 92.

3. Hooper, p. 92.

4. Thanks to Andrew Tucker for this point.

Fig. 166 Ties manufactured by Welch, Margetson & Company illustrated in their 1903 catalogue. Neckwear and collars were made at the company's factory in Bermondsey.

INDEX

Page numbers in italics refer to figure captions